The Late Middle Ages

Philip Daileader, Ph.D.

THE
GREAT
COURSES

PUBLISHED BY:

THE GREAT COURSES
Corporate Headquarters
4840 Westfields Boulevard, Suite 500
Chantilly, Virginia 20151-2299
Phone: 1-800-832-2412
Fax: 703-378-3819
www.thegreatcourses.com

Copyright © The Teaching Company, 2007

Printed in the United States of America

This book is in copyright. All rights reserved.

Without limiting the rights under copyright reserved above,
no part of this publication may be reproduced, stored in
or introduced into a retrieval system, or transmitted,
in any form, or by any means
(electronic, mechanical, photocopying, recording, or otherwise),
without the prior written permission of
The Teaching Company.

Philip Daileader, Ph.D.

Associate Professor of History, The College of William and Mary

Philip Daileader is Associate Professor of History at The College of William and Mary in Virginia. He received his B.A. in History from The Johns Hopkins University in 1990, where he was elected to the Phi Beta Kappa Honor Society. He received his M.A. and his Ph.D. in History from Harvard University in 1991 and 1996, respectively.

While a graduate student at Harvard, he was a four-time winner of the Harvard University Certificate of Distinction in Teaching. At William and Mary, he has been awarded an Alumni Fellowship Teaching Award (2004) and the College's Phi Beta Kappa Teaching Award (2005). He currently holds one of the school's University Chairs in Teaching Excellence. Before coming to William and Mary, he taught at the State University of New York at New Paltz and the University of Alabama.

Dr. Daileader's research focuses on the social, cultural, and religious history of Mediterranean Europe. His first book, *True Citizens: Violence, Memory, and Identity in the Medieval Community of Perpignan, 1162–1397*, was published by Brill Academic Publishers in 2000 and appeared in French translation in 2004. His articles include "One Will, One Voice, and Equal Love: Papal Elections and the *Liber Pontificalis* in the Early Middle Ages," published in *Archivum Historiae Pontificiae*; "The Vanishing Consulates of Catalonia" published in *Speculum*; and "*La coutume dans un pays aux trois religions: Catalogne, 1229–1319*" ("Custom in a Land of Three Religions: Catalonia, 1229–1319") published in *Annales du Midi*. Presently he is working on a biographical study of St. Vincent Ferrar (c. 1350–1419).

The Late Middle Ages is his third course for The Teaching Company. The first, *The High Middle Ages*, was released in 2001 and the second, *The Early Middle Ages*, was released in 2004.

Table of Contents
The Late Middle Ages

Table of Contents
The Late Middle Ages

The Late Middle Ages

Scope:

Few historical periods present as many apparent contradictions as do the Late Middle Ages, conventionally defined as lasting from c. 1300 to c. 1500. It is, on the one hand, an age that experiences disasters and tragedies of such magnitude that those who survive them cannot remember the like and doubt that subsequent generations will be capable of believing their descriptions of what happened. Chief among these disasters is the coming of the Black Death in 1347 and 1348, which kills perhaps one-half of the European population in the space of four years and remains a constant presence for centuries to come. Compounding the shock caused by such loss of human life is war, especially the Hundred Years War; religious turmoil, brought about by King Philip the Fair's trial of the Templars and humiliation of the papacy, by the long residence of popes at Avignon rather than at Rome, and by the Great Papal Schism of 1378–1417; and the threat of urban and rural revolt, which sometimes takes on aggressively apocalyptic and millenarian overtones.

Yet at the very moment that Europe is reeling from its losses, a new intellectual and cultural movement arises, Humanism, which emphasizes the enormous human capacity for goodness, creativity, and happiness—happiness achieved not just in the next world through salvation but in this world.

The tension and dynamic generated by this unexpected optimism in the face of catastrophe help to make the Late Middle Ages so interesting. It is a period when much that we regard as medieval and much that we regard as modern come to coexist for a time—sometimes uneasily. The Late Middle Ages is still an age of knights, serfs, and castles but also an age of cannon and muskets. Scholastic theologians such as William Ockham, John Wycliffe, and Jan Hus, ponder the nature of God and God's methods for saving humanity, while Humanist artists and authors proclaim humanity itself to be the proper object of study. The Humanists of the Italian Renaissance revive Classical values even as the Byzantine Empire, the direct continuation of the eastern half of the Roman Empire, finally collapses and Columbus's voyage of exploration demonstrates that the revered intellectual authorities of the ancient world knew less than was commonly supposed. And the innovations and inventions of the late-medieval world cannot simply be lumped together as "progress," because the same period that gives rise to the printing press also gives rise to the Spanish Inquisition (an intimidating institution, even if its lurid reputation is not always deserved) and to the first European witch trials.

Not surprisingly, given the strong cross-currents that swirl through our period, those historians who have written most influentially and evocatively about the years from 1300 to 1500—the 19th-century Swiss historian Jacob Burckhardt, the early-20th-century Dutch historian Johan Huizinga, and the Pulitzer Prize–winning American historian Barbara Tuchman—have created rather different portraits of the age, sometimes emphasizing its modernism and sometimes its medievalism; sometimes seeing it as a period of rebirth, sometimes of waning or of calamity. One of the goals of this course is to consider whether Burckhardt's, Huizinga's, or Tuchman's vision of this period is the most accurate—or whether the Late Middle Ages ought to be considered a period of rebirth, waning, *and* calamity, or whether the most crucial aspects of the Late Middle Ages need to be defined and characterized in a wholly different manner.

This course is intended to familiarize students with the period's major events, personalities, and developments to provide the material with which to formulate their own ideas about the nature of the Late Middle Ages. The course proceeds roughly chronologically. The first nine lectures discuss specific events dating to the 14th century and the first half of the 15th century: for example, the trial of the Templars, the Babylonian Captivity of the papacy and the Great Papal Schism, the Hundred Years War, the Black Death, and the English Peasants Revolt of 1381. The next nine lectures focus less on specific events and more on the lives of individuals, such as William Ockham, John Wycliffe, Jan Hus, Christine de Pizan, and Catherine of Siena, who place their stamp on the intellectual, literary, and religious life of the age. These nine middle lectures also examine developments that arise not at a single identifiable moment but gradually during the course of the Late Middle Ages: witch trials, gunpowder weapons, printing, and Humanism. The concluding six lectures return to the approach of the opening lectures and treat major events during the second half of the 15th century: the fall of the Byzantine Empire, the marriage of Ferdinand and Isabella, the establishment of the Spanish Inquisition, and Columbus's first voyage to the Americas.

The designation *Late Middle Ages* suggests that the Middle Ages, in some sense, comes to an end between 1300 and 1500. The concluding lecture will take a look back at the Late Middle Ages and at the Middle Ages as a whole; in doing so, it will make a case for the proposition that by 1500, the Middle Ages was far from over. Rather, the period of the Late Middle Ages merely lays the groundwork for a fundamental break with the medieval past that occurs only centuries later—and much more recently than is commonly supposed.

Lecture One
Late Middle Ages—Rebirth, Waning, Calamity?

Scope: During the 14th and 15th centuries, Italian Humanists came to believe that they were living either at the tail end of, or just after, the Middle Ages, which they understood as a period of literary and artistic decline, unlike the cultural revival, or Renaissance, to which the Humanists themselves aspired. Eminent and influential modern historians such as Jacob Burckhardt, Johan Huizinga, and Barbara Tuchman have disagreed as to whether the 14th and 15th centuries—designated as the *Late Middle Ages* by modern historians—should be regarded as a grim age of catastrophe or as a bright age of newfound creativity and optimism, as more medieval than modern or more modern than medieval. This course focuses on the major personalities and events of the period, which will help us to assess whether the 14th and 15th centuries indeed mark the decisive turning point between the medieval and the modern and whether these centuries constituted a high or a low point in European history.

Outline

I. Compared to the Early Middle Ages (c. 300–1000) and the High Middle Ages (c. 1000–1300), the Late Middle Ages (c. 1300–1500) is, in some ways, the most difficult part of the Middle Ages to study.

   A. The concept of the Middle Ages emerged during the 14th and 15th centuries among Italian Humanists, who initially thought themselves to be living in the Middle Ages but came to believe that they were, in fact, living in a new and different era.

   B. Literacy rates were relatively high, but the printing press was not invented until near the end of the period; thus, there survive from the 14th and 15th centuries an overwhelming mass of handwritten documents, many of which have yet to be examined by historians.

   C. Historians have found it difficult to organize themselves efficiently for the study of a period whose identity, split between the Renaissance and the Middle Ages, is so problematic.

II. Of the three historians whose writings have most powerfully shaped modern conceptions of the Late Middle Ages, Jacob Burckhardt (1819–1897) is perhaps the most influential of them all.

    A. Burckhardt came from the town of Basel, Switzerland. He studied history at the University of Berlin under Leopold von Ranke, probably the most important historian produced by Europe in the 19th century.

    B. Burckhardt published his first book, *The Age of Constantine the Great*, in 1853, and his masterpiece, *The Civilization of the Renaissance in Italy*, in 1860. So great was Burckhardt's reputation after the publication of *The Civilization of the Renaissance in Italy* that he was invited to be Ranke's successor in Berlin—an invitation that he declined.

    C. Burckhardt depicted 14th- and 15th-century Italy as the birthplace of modernity because, in Burckhardt's view, the Italian Renaissance reintroduced to Europe the value of individualism: The maximizing of the human potential of each individual became a cultural ideal, as did the unabashed pursuit of personal fame and glory.

    D. Although Burckhardt was sure that modernity had emerged in 14th- and 15th-century Italy, he was ambivalent as to whether that was good or bad for humanity. He admired the artistic productions of the Italian Renaissance and had no desire to return to the Middle Ages; however, he was hostile to democracy and 19th-century political developments in general and, thus, regarded the Renaissance as partially to blame for ushering in the age of mass politics and mass society.

    E. Especially in North America, readers emphasized and identified with Burckhardt's depiction of a dynamic and modernizing 14th and 15th centuries, while jettisoning his trepidation about where modernity was leading. Thus, Burckhardt's view of the Renaissance came to be understood as more one-sidedly celebratory than, in fact, it was.

III. If any book has come close to rivaling the influence and reputation of Burckhardt's *Civilization of the Renaissance in Italy*, that book is Johan Huizinga's *The Waning of the Middle Ages*, first published in 1919, translated into English in 1924, then translated again, under the title *The Autumn of the Middle Ages*, in 1996.

A. Huizinga (1872–1945) was a Dutch historian whose formal academic training was as a philologist specializing in Sanskrit. He wrote voluminously (unlike Burckhardt, who never published a major scholarly work during the final 37 years of his life) on a range of topics, from ancient India to the modern Netherlands.

B. Huizinga greatly admired Burckhardt, and in several important respects, Huizinga's work resembles Burckhardt's.

    1. Like Burckhardt, Huizinga was interested primarily in cultural history, especially the history of art and literature but also popular culture.

    2. Like Burckhardt, Huizinga approached his subject matter idiosyncratically, discussing topics that interested him and ignoring seemingly important topics that did not.

C. Despite the similarities, Huizinga's *Waning of the Middle Ages*, written with an evocative power seldom matched since, was a rejoinder to Burckhardt's book.

    1. Huizinga focused on Europe north of the Alps, especially the Burgundian Netherlands.

    2. Huizinga saw the 14th and 15th centuries as more medieval than modern, and he emphasized the differences between culture and everyday life as they existed in the Late Middle Ages and in his own day.

    3. Huizinga saw the 14th and 15th centuries as a period when medieval European culture was "overripe." Although the cultural ideals and tendencies of the medieval period, such as chivalry or allegorical thinking, remained ubiquitous, they had increasingly little to do with the realities of the day.

IV. Barbara Tuchman (1912–1989) is the 20th-century historian whose English-language book on the Late Middle Ages, called *A Distant Mirror: The Calamitous Fourteenth Century* and published in 1978, has enjoyed the greatest readership.

A. Unlike Burckhardt and Huizinga, Tuchman was not an academic historian.

    1. She came from a wealthy family of national political importance.

    2. She wrote historical narratives that examined events roughly in the order in which they occurred.

      3.   In explaining why historical events happened as they did, Tuchman pointed to the character, intellect, and personality quirks of individual leaders.

    B.   Tuchman turned from 20th-century history to the history of the Late Middle Ages because she felt herself and the contemporary world to be living in the "shadow of calamity," and she wished to examine how humans had responded to calamity in the past.

    C.   Like Burckhardt, Tuchman emphasized similarities between the 14th and 15th centuries, on the one hand, and her own times, on the other, and perceived the emergence of modernity during this period. Like Huizinga, though, she focused on Europe north of the Alps and on the grimness of the times.

V.   This course examines the major events of the 14th and 15th centuries in the hope that a greater familiarity with the events of this period will allow us to address the central issues raised by Burckhardt, Huizinga, Tuchman, and others: Did the Middle Ages end and modernity begin during the 14th and 15th centuries, and did the 14th and 15th centuries constitute an era of disaster or of efflorescence?

Suggested Readings:

Jacob Burckhardt, *The Civilization of the Renaissance in Italy.*

Johan Huizinga, *The Autumn of the Middle Ages* and *The Waning of the Middle Ages.*

Anthony Molho, "The Italian Renaissance, Made in the USA."

Barbara Tuchman, *A Distant Mirror: The Calamitous Fourteenth Century.*

Questions to Consider:

1.   When studying a period such as the Late Middle Ages, what role should the present and the more recent past play in the study of the more distant past? Should historians use their knowledge of subsequent events to determine what was important in the period under consideration? Should historians take each period on its own terms, blocking out (insofar as they can) their knowledge of more recent history, lest that knowledge lead to anachronism?

2.   Would it be possible or desirable for historians to stop using blanket terms, such as *Middle Ages* and *Renaissance*, to describe long periods of history?

Lecture Two
Philip the Fair versus Boniface VIII

Scope: At the outset of the Late Middle Ages, a fierce conflict erupted between the chief spiritual authority in Christian Europe, the pope, and one of Europe's leading monarchs, the king of France. Although conflicts between religious and secular leaders were hardly unprecedented, the struggle between Pope Boniface VIII and King Philip IV of France differed from earlier, high-medieval conflicts in that it arose from royal, not papal, initiatives. It differed, too, in its outcome. Whereas the papacy had largely held its own against secular authorities in the High Middle Ages, at this time, Philip IV got his way on all the most important issues. Philip IV's victory over Boniface VIII resulted in a weakened papacy and a growth of French influence; both of these factors would shape the religious history of 14th-century Europe.

Outline

I. By 1300, the French monarchy had grown so powerful that King Philip IV (also known as Philip the Fair) felt himself capable of testing the extent of papal authority within his kingdom. The pope whom Philip IV challenged, Boniface VIII, was in several respects ill-suited to defend ecclesiastical prerogative against the French monarchy.

    A. Boniface VIII had been elected under strange circumstances. His predecessor, a revered hermit who took the name Celestine V, had resigned the papal office. It was not clear whether Celestine V had the legal right to do this, which in turn, raised questions about the legitimacy of Boniface VIII's election.

    B. Boniface VIII, who seems to have encouraged Celestine V to step down, further invited criticism by having the former pope arrested and held in confinement until Celestine V's death in 1296.

II. Philip IV of France challenged papal authority by claiming that French kings had the right to tax the clergy of the kingdom without first securing papal consent to such taxation.

    A. In 1215, the Fourth Lateran Council had established the principle that kings could not tax the clergy without papal permission.

B. When war broke out between France and England in 1294, Philip IV had a French church council authorize taxation of the clergy, but he failed to get papal approval for the tax.

C. Boniface VIII responded with a papal bull, *Clericis laicos*, issued in 1296, that reasserted the ruling of the Fourth Lateran Council. After the French king imposed an economic blockade on the papacy, though, Boniface VIII capitulated and permitted the taxation.

III. Even though Philip IV had secured the right to tax his kingdom's clergy without the pope's permission, he continued to challenge Boniface VIII on a number of other issues. These challenges led Boniface VIII to assert that within Europe, the spiritual authority of the pope was superior to the secular authority of any monarch—an assertion that Philip IV disputed violently.

A. In 1301, after Philip IV had arrested a bishop, Boniface VIII forbade the French clergy to pay any more taxes to the French king. The pope also summoned Philip IV to a council in Rome that would judge whether Philip IV should remain in office.

B. In 1302, Philip IV assembled a council of his own at Paris. Attended by nobles, clergy, and commoners, this council was the first meeting of what would become the French Estates General. At the Estates General, Philip IV called upon his subjects to stand with him against the pope, whose legitimacy he questioned.

C. In November 1302, Boniface VIII released the papal bull *Unam sanctam*, which stated concisely and unequivocally that popes should judge the suitability of kings for their office, not vice versa.

D. In 1303, Philip IV repeated his claim that Boniface VIII was not a legitimate pope and added a string of sensational accusations: that Boniface VIII was a heretic, a murderer, a sodomite, and a devil worshipper.

IV. Matters between Boniface VIII and Philip IV came to a head in September 1303, when the king's representatives kidnapped the pope.

A. A rumor was circulating, quite possibly true, that on September 8, 1303, Boniface VIII planned to excommunicate Philip IV and declare him to be deposed.

B. On the 7th of September, one of the king's advisors, Guillaume de Nogaret, together with members of the Colonna family (who disliked Boniface VIII), entered the town of Anagni, where the pope was staying. They demanded that the pope leave with them as their prisoner. When the pope refused, they stormed the building where the pope was staying and took him captive.

C. After the kidnappers fell out among themselves regarding what to do with the pope, residents of Anagni attacked the captors and freed the pope on September 9.

V. Although Boniface VIII had been held captive for just two days, the event had repercussions.

A. Across Europe, responses to the attack at Anagni were fairly muted. Some individuals, such as Dante, denounced Philip IV, but others blamed Boniface VIII for bringing the misfortune on himself.

B. In having Boniface VIII seized—and this pope died the very next month, supposedly of shock—the French king showed his willingness to employ any tactic in his struggle with the papacy.

C. Philip the Fair's reputation for aggressiveness caused Boniface VIII's successors, Benedict XI and, especially, Clement V, to take a more conciliatory approach.

Suggested Readings:

Francis Oakley, *The Western Church in the Later Middle Ages*.

Joseph Strayer, *The Reign of Philip the Fair*.

Questions to Consider:

1. If you had been alive in 1300, whose side would you have taken in the struggle between Boniface VIII and Philip IV? Whose side should you have taken?

2. Given how intertwined European religious and political life were in the 1300s and, given that our concepts of church and state might not match up with those concepts as they existed in 1300, should the conflict between Boniface VIII and Philip IV be understood as a struggle between "church" and "state"?

Lecture Three
Fall of the Templars and the Avignon Papacy

Scope: During the pontificates of Boniface VIII's successors, King Philip IV of France continued to defy papal authority and to pressure the papacy. After the archbishop of Bordeaux was elected as Pope Clement V in 1305, he never traveled to Rome but, instead, remained in the south of France. Shortly after that, Philip IV arrested and put on trial the French members of the Order of the Temple, medieval Europe's most prestigious military order and one that was supposedly accountable to the papacy. As of 1309, Avignon, not Rome, was the seat of the papacy, and it remained so until 1377. The Italian Humanist Petrarch invented the name by which this prolonged absence of the papacy from Rome and Italy would subsequently be known: the *Babylonian Captivity*. Foreigners exaggerated somewhat the extent of French influence over the papacy at this time, but there was certainly the perception that the papacy had been Frenchified, and that perception could only diminish the authority of an institution that aspired to universality.

Outline

I. When the archbishop of Bordeaux was elected as Pope Clement V in 1305, he never traveled to Rome but, instead, remained in the south of France—his papal coronation took place at Lyon.

   A. Clement V's decision to stay in the south of France was not so much the result of French pressure as of short-term papal interest.

   1. Clement V wanted to resolve disputes between France and England over the ownership of Aquitaine, in the southwest of modern France, because such disputes prevented kings from leaving their kingdoms and taking part in crusades. After the fall of the last crusader state in 1291, Clement V was interested in organizing a new crusade to regain lost territory.

   2. Further, violent struggles among Rome's leading families left the city in such disorder that Clement V feared to go there.

    B. Even though Clement V's residence in the south of France was voluntary, he attempted to placate Philip IV by revoking the papal bulls *Unam sanctam* and *Clericis laicos.*

II. Philip IV followed up his attack on the pope at Anagni with an even more spectacular act of defiance: the seizure and trial of the Knights Templar.

    A. Founded in 1119 in the aftermath of the First Crusade, the Knights Templar constituted medieval Europe's most prestigious and wealthy military order.

        1. A military order is one whose members are both monks and warriors. Like monks, they live in a common house, following the precepts of a written rule; they lead austere lives; and they take specific vows.

        2. Unlike monks, they continue to fight like knights, only now on behalf of Christianity against its enemies.

    B. Legally, Templars answered only to the papacy, but by the reign of Philip the Fair, the order was widely criticized for its wealth and its failure to keep or to recapture Jerusalem.

    C. Precisely why Philip the Fair ordered the investigation and arrest of all of France's Templars remains an open question.

        1. He may have genuinely believed rumors that the Templars secretly held heretical beliefs and engaged in shocking blaspheming rituals.

        2. He may have seen this arrest as a way of further humiliating the papacy.

        3. He may have been interested primarily in seizing the Templars' property; Joseph Strayer, the leading historian of Philip the Fair, inclined toward this view.

    D. In 1307, after the pope had failed to move against the Templars to Philip IV's satisfaction, Philip IV ordered the arrest of all the Templars in France and the sequestering of their property.

    E. Between 1307 and 1311, Philip IV conducted trials of the French Templars, a number of whom confessed (after being tortured) to the crimes of which they were accused. Finally, in 1312, Pope Clement V ordered that all Templar houses throughout Europe should be disbanded.

F. Clement V was much criticized for the dissolution of the Templars, but Philip IV had exerted substantial pressure on Clement V to proclaim that Boniface VIII had been a heretic; Clement V may have given in on the issue of the Templars in order to gain a bargaining chip in his discussions over the posthumous fate of Boniface VIII.

III. In 1309, Clement V moved to Avignon, which would remain the seat of the papacy until 1377.

    A. There seems not to have been a single decision to keep the papacy at Avignon, but a series of coincidences and improvised reactions to new events, such as the outbreak of the Hundred Years War between France and England in 1337, worked to keep the popes at Avignon.

    B. It had not been unusual for popes to travel outside Rome; indeed, since 1100, popes had spent more time outside Rome than in it. It was unprecedented, however, for popes to make their permanent residence outside Italy.

    C. Outside France, there was growing sentiment that the pope should return to Italy and to Rome—after all, papal primacy rested on the fact that popes were the bishops of Rome and, therefore, the successors of Saint Peter.

        1. This pressure on the papacy did not come just from Italy, but it was expressed most forcefully there.

        2. The Italian Humanist Petrarch, who portrayed the papal court in Avignon as depraved, used the phrase *Babylonian Captivity* to describe the papacy's absence from his beloved Rome.

    D. By the 1360s, inertia and the size of the papal court had made it difficult for the papacy to return to Rome. Although there was an attempt to move the papacy back to Rome in 1367, not until 1377 did the papacy return there once and for all.

    E. In 1378, the first papal election to occur in Rome in nearly three generations was held. Rioters demanded that the cardinals elect a Roman or, at least, an Italian, which the cardinals did. This new pope, Urban VI, was the first Italian elected as pope in nearly 75 years.

Suggested Readings:

Malcolm Barber, *The Trial of the Templars*, 2nd ed.

Sophia Menache, *Clement V*.

Yves Renouard, *The Avignon Papacy, 1305–1403*.

Questions to Consider:

1. Why have the Templars and the trial of the Templars been the subjects of so much historical writing, much of it conspiratorial?

2. Of all the defeats and setbacks experienced by the 14th-century papacy, which was the most harmful to the institution? Why?

Lecture Four
The Great Papal Schism

Scope: In 1378, shortly after the return of the papacy to Rome from Avignon, two papal elections were held under unusual conditions. As a result, two different men, Urban VI (who remained in Rome) and Clement VII (who returned to Avignon), each claimed to be the legitimate pope and enjoyed substantial support in Europe. The result was the Great Papal Schism, which lasted for some 40 years, from 1378 to 1417. During this time, rival lines of popes existed at Rome and at Avignon, splitting Christian Europe for nearly two generations. One consequence of the Great Papal Schism was the emergence of the conciliar movement, which sought to make general councils, rather than the papacy, the supreme religious authority within the Christian Church. Although such councils played a decisive role in ending the schism, they failed to supplant the papacy, largely because popes outmaneuvered conciliarists during the course of the 15th century.

Outline

I. In 1378, the College of Cardinals convened at Rome and elected an Italian as Pope Urban VI. Later that same year, a group of French cardinals who had participated in the election of Urban VI held another election and chose a Frenchman, Clement VII, who moved to Avignon in 1379.

   A. The French cardinals justified their election of Clement VII by arguing that they had elected Urban VI under duress, which made the election invalid.

   B. However, because only a splinter group of cardinals participated in the election of Clement VII, his election was at least as open to challenge as Urban VI's had been.

   C. Both Urban VI and Clement VII enjoyed widespread support in Europe, with traditional allies favoring the same pope and traditional rivals favoring rival popes. Thus, France and France's allies (Scotland, Castile) supported Clement VII, while England and Germany supported Urban VI.

    D. Within each kingdom, though, both popes could find supporters, and individual towns and religious orders sometimes split into competing camps, each of which supported one of the two popes.

    E. Even after Urban VI and Clement VII died, their supporters refused to acknowledge the legitimacy of the rival pope and, instead, elected successors for their own popes. As a result, rival lines of popes emerged at Rome and at Avignon; even the intervention of monarchs around 1400 failed to convince one or both of these popes to step down.

II. General councils had long played an important role in the history of the Christian Church. When the Great Papal Schism left contemporaries uncertain whether the popes at Avignon or the popes at Rome were the legitimate heads of the church, some thinkers argued that the authority of such councils was superior to that of popes. This point of view was known as *conciliarism*.

    A. Shortly after the outbreak of the Great Papal Schism, some theologians argued that only a church council could legitimately determine the true pope.

    B. Some theologians saw conciliarism not just as a solution to a temporary problem but as a principle that should endure even after the end of the Great Papal Schism. Because general councils represented the whole church, while popes represented just the local church of Rome, conciliar superiority existed even when there was just one pope. These conciliarists demanded that the meeting of general councils become regular and mandatory.

III. As the Great Papal Schism dragged on, the conciliar movement gained ground, and a series of important church councils (one of which succeeded in ending the Great Papal Schism) gave the impression that general councils might well replace the papacy as the head of the church.

    A. At the Council of Pisa in 1409, a group of cardinals proclaimed the popes at Rome and Avignon to be deposed and elected a new pope, Alexander V, to replace them. Neither the pope at Avignon nor the pope at Rome recognized the legitimacy of the Council of Pisa, though; as a result, Christian Europe now had three competing popes, worsening the Schism. [Alexander V, who died in 1410, was succeeded in Pisa by John XXIII, who is considered an antipope or false claimant. When Cardinal Angelo Giuseppe Roncalli was elected pope in 1958, he took the name John XXIII.]

B. The council that finally succeeded in ending the Great Papal Schism was the Council of Constance, which ran from 1414 to 1417.

    1. The Council of Constance was summoned by the Holy Roman Emperor and (begrudgingly) by the pope at Pisa.

    2. Although the pope at Pisa withdrew his support for the Council, it remained in session and, in 1415, proclaimed that all Christians, even popes, were bound to abide by its decisions.

    3. The Council of Constance deposed or wrangled resignations from all three sitting popes and induced nearly all the supporters of these three popes to withdraw their allegiance to them. Once all three popes were removed from power, the cardinals elected a new single pope, Martin V, in 1417.

    4. Before adjourning, the Council of Constance decreed that similar councils should meet routinely in the future and that popes had no right to prevent such meetings.

IV. The Council of Constance marked the high point of the conciliar movement. During the rest of the 15th century, Pope Martin V and his successors regained the power that the papacy had lost to councils during the Great Papal Schism.

A. At the Council of Basel in 1431, the pope attempted, at first unsuccessfully, to force the Council to disband.

B. The pope was able to drive a wedge among the conciliarists and split the Council, however, when he ordered the Council to move to Italy in response to an unexpected development: the appearance of Byzantine ambassadors offering to negotiate the reunion of the Catholic and the Orthodox Christian Churches.

    1. The Byzantine ambassadors wanted the negotiations to take place in Italy rather than in relatively distant Switzerland.

    2. In 1437, the pope ordered the Council of Basel to disband and reconvene in Italy. Most members of the Council refused and remained in session. Some, however, accepted the legitimacy of the order and opened their own council in Italy, first at Ferrara, then at Florence. As a result, as of 1437, two rival and schismatic councils were in session.

3. After the Council of Basel failed to depose the pope and lost popular support, it disbanded itself in 1449, marking a defeat for the conciliar movement.

4. In 1460, the pope underscored the superiority of the papacy vis-à-vis councils by proclaiming, in the papal bull *Execrabilis*, that no one could appeal a papal ruling to a council.

Suggested Readings:

Renate Blumenfeld-Kosinski, *Poets, Saints, and Visionaries of the Great Schism, 1378–1417.*

Francis Oakley, *The Conciliarist Tradition: Constitutionalism in the Catholic Church, 1300–1870.*

Brian Tierney, *Foundations of the Conciliar Theory.*

Questions to Consider:

1. Would the subsequent religious history of Europe have been markedly different if conciliarism had triumphed in the 15th century? If so, how?

2. To what extent was the defeat of conciliarism the result of a chance event (the appearance of the Byzantine ambassadors), and to what extent was it likely under any circumstances that the conciliar movement would fail?

Lecture Five
The Hundred Years War, Part 1

Scope: The political history of 14th-century Europe was dominated by the Hundred Years War between France and England. Relations between the two kingdoms had been complex and often strained ever since the Norman conquest of England in 1066, and the two countries were frequently at war during the High Middle Ages. Nevertheless, the Hundred Years War differed from its predecessors in its length (it ran, off and on, from 1337 to 1453), in the types of weapons and armies used, and in its purpose. The war soon centered on a far-reaching issue: whether or not the king of England's claim to the French throne would be recognized by the French. During the first phase of the Hundred Years War, English successes brought the king of England closer to his goal and touched off a violent peasant revolt in France, the *Jacquerie*. Although England consolidated its gains in the Treaty of Brétigny in 1360, this treaty marked only a pause in the fighting.

Outline

I. The concept of the Hundred Years War is a problematic one, which historians use largely out of convenience.

   A. The phrase both overstates the reality of the conflict (there were long periods of truce during the Hundred Years War and the fighting was not continuous) and understates it (the war lasted for more than 100 years).

   B. The phrase *Hundred Years War* did not appear until the 19th century, when contemporary scholars assessed the war as a continuation of previous struggles between France and England over issues rooted in the Norman conquest of 1066 and its aftermath.

   C. Indeed, the Hundred Years War was the outcome of problems that had existed for more than two centuries.

   1. Ever since the conquest of England by the duke of Normandy in 1066, English kings were simultaneously the equals of the kings of France (in their capacity as monarchs) and vassals of the kings of France (in their capacity as dukes of Normandy).

2. By 1154, kings of England controlled the western half of France. French kings subsequently whittled down English holdings there yet, as of 1259, English kings still remained in control of Gascony (in the southwest of France) and retained the title "duke of Aquitaine." By virtue of this land and title, they also continued to be vassals of the kings of France.

II. Although the Hundred Years War arose over a specific incident that was itself fairly minor, it soon became a war about whether the Kingdom of France would remain independent of English rule.

A. In 1337, the king of France proclaimed that the king of England had forfeited his right to Gascony by failing to perform his vassalic duties properly. France then attacked Gascony in the hope of confiscating the fief from England.

B. Nine years earlier, in 1328, the Capetian dynasty in France had died out, and different candidates had claimed the French throne.
   1. One Frenchman, Philip of Valois, was embraced by the French and became Philip VI.
   2. Edward III, king of England, had a good claim to the French throne, too. He dropped the claim in response to a lack of French enthusiasm, but after the Hundred Years War broke out, he revived his claim to the French throne, took the title "king of France" for himself in 1340, and proclaimed Philip of Valois to be a usurper, thereby raising the stakes significantly.

III. The first phase of the Hundred Years War lasted until the Treaty of Brétigny, signed in 1360. During this phase, English successes left the Kingdom of France in a weak bargaining position.

A. By allying with Flanders and seizing French ports on the English Channel, Edward III established bases from which he could easily raid into France.

B. Instead of trying to capture and hold territory, Edward III relied on destructive hit-and-run forays, called *chevauchées*, to break the will of the French to resist, and avoided pitched battles.

C. On two occasions, French armies caught up with retreating English raiding parties, and on both occasions—the Battle of Crécy in 1346 and the Battle of Poitiers in 1356—the English badly defeated the French.

D. At the Battle of Poitiers in 1356, the English took the king of France prisoner.

IV. After the French defeat at Poitiers and the capture of the French king by the English, revolts broke out in Paris and the countryside around Paris. The revolt of the French peasants around Paris is called the *Jacquerie*.

    A. In 1357, Parisians, under the leadership of a merchant named Etienne Marcel, revolted against the French royal government and seized control of Paris.

    B. In May 1358, peasants in the countryside around Paris began attacking and killing nobles, sacking their castles and homes wherever possible with a violence that made a deep impression on contemporaries.

    C. Etienne Marcel and the Parisians allied with the peasants of the *Jacquerie*, but by the middle of June, French nobles had rallied and put down the *Jacquerie* with great force. The inhabitants of Paris then turned against Marcel and killed him later that summer.

V. After the capture of the king of France and the *Jacquerie*, the French government had little choice but to negotiate with the king of England. The result of these negotiations was the Treaty of Brétigny, signed in 1360, which was very favorable to England—but not quite as favorable as one might have expected under the circumstances.

    A. The Treaty of Brétigny contained much that the king of England wanted.

        1. England was allowed to keep most of the French territory that it had captured, including the strategically important port of Calais in the north of France.

        2. Kings of England were no longer to be considered vassals of the kings of France.

        3. France would have to pay an enormous ransom to England to secure the release of the French king.

    B. For his part, the king of England agreed to renounce his claims to the French throne.

    C. Despite this concession on the part of the English king, many in France wanted revenge for the damages they had suffered during the opening decades of the war, and it would not be long before the Hundred Years War resumed.

Suggested Readings:

Christopher Allmand, *The Hundred Years War: England and France at War, c. 1300–c. 1450*.

Anne Curry, *The Hundred Years War*, 2nd ed.

Jonathan Sumption, *The Hundred Years War*.

Questions to Consider:

1. Which other military conflicts in European history does the Hundred Years War most resemble?

2. If the king of England had made good his claim to the French throne during the Hundred Years War, how might the subsequent history of Europe been different?

Lecture Six
The Hundred Years War, Part 2

Scope: The Treaty of Brétigny, signed by the kings of France and England
in 1360, marked only a brief pause in the Hundred Years War.
Both sides failed to abide by its terms; thus, the war resumed in
1369, the year in which the king of England renewed his claim to
the French throne. After the decisive English victory at the Battle
of Agincourt in 1415 and a string of other successes, the English
king came very close to acquiring the French crown for his heir.
The unexpected appearance and intervention of Joan of Arc,
however, enabled France to maintain its independence and, after
Joan's death, drive the English almost entirely from French
territory. In addition to its geopolitical ramifications, the Hundred
Years War was significant for the changes in military technology
and organization it fostered. The Hundred Years War
demonstrated the effectiveness of the longbow against knights and
contributed to the emergence of larger, infantry-based armies—a
trend that would have political and social repercussions of its own.

Outline

I. The Hundred Years War resumed in 1369 after a decade of mutual
provocation (especially by the French). After a series of French
victories, France and England signed a second truce, in 1396, on terms
somewhat favorable to France.

    A. During the 1360s, both sides had failed to abide by the provisions
of the Treaty of Brétigny. War broke out after France resumed
treating the kings of England as their vassals and after the king of
England resumed the use of the title "king of France."

    B. During this second phase of the war, France began raiding the
English coast and reoccupied much of Aquitaine.

    C. The truce signed by England and France in 1396 left unresolved
the most important questions—the English claim to the French
throne and the status of Aquitaine. That, combined with England's
desire to avenge the defeats it had suffered, fueled the resumption
of the war in 1415.

II. Between 1415 and 1429, the king of England nearly succeeded in acquiring the French crown.

    A. In 1415, the English invaded Normandy. Instead of relying on hit-and-run raids, as they had done earlier in the war, the English pursued a strategy of systematic and permanent conquest: besieging major towns, exiling natives, and bringing in English settlers.

    B. At the Battle of Agincourt in 1415, a large army of French knights suffered a defeat as severe as those experienced at Crécy and Poitiers earlier in the war.

    C. In 1420, King Charles VI of France signed the Treaty of Troyes, which stated that after the death of Charles VI, the next king of France should not be Charles's own son but the son of King Henry V of England.

    D. Both Charles VI of France and Henry V of England died in 1422. French resistance to the Treaty of Troyes remained strong, however, and fighting broke out again as England tried to make good the claim of the nine-month-old Henry VI to the French throne.

    E. After a series of English victories, Henry VI was crowned king of France in 1431, but his coronation was rejected in France—indeed, by the time of his coronation, the tide had begun to swing decisively against the English.

III. Only the unusual intervention of Joan of Arc allowed France to halt the English advance and push back the English. When the Hundred Years War finally came to an end in 1453, England had lost nearly all of its French territory.

    A. Joan was born around 1412. From the age of 13, she had experienced religious visions; when she was about 16, voices instructed her to travel to, and meet with, the *dauphin*, or French heir to the throne, whom she was to assist in recapturing his kingdom.

    B. In 1429, Joan of Arc traveled to, and met with, the son of Charles VI. He permitted her to lead French troops and rescue Orléans, then Reims, the traditional site of French royal coronations.

    C. After these victories, the son of Charles VI had himself crowned as Charles VII, king of France, in 1429.

D. When Joan of Arc was captured by the Burgundians, Charles VII failed to ransom her, perhaps because he was uncomfortable with the fact that a cross-dressing peasant girl had won the throne for him. The Burgundians instead ransomed Joan of Arc to the English, who burned her as a witch in 1431.

E. Despite the death of Joan of Arc, France continued to push the English out of French territory. By 1453, when the war effectively ended, England had lost all its French possessions other than the port of Calais.

IV. The Hundred Years War fostered important changes in how kingdoms fought wars and how they paid for those wars. In the long run, these changes strengthened monarchical power in both France and England.

    A. The Hundred Years War made direct national taxation a common event.

        1. Before the Hundred Years War, kings could levy kingdom-wide direct taxes only in cases of great emergency. Under ordinary circumstances, kings were to finance the royal government from indirect taxes and, most especially, from their own financial resources.

        2. The Hundred Years War left both France and England in a nearly permanent state of emergency; thus, the collection of kingdom-wide direct taxes, perhaps a once-a-decade event in England before the Hundred Years War, became, on average, a biannual event that persisted even during times of peace.

    B. Kings used the greater financial resources at their disposal to pay for armies that were larger and relied increasingly on foot soldiers, hired to fight for the duration of specific campaigns.

        1. The increased reliance on paid foot soldiers hired for specific campaigns made the Hundred Years War that much more devastating. During periods of truce and, therefore, unemployment, mercenary bands pillaged civilian populations.

        2. Around 1450, France addressed the problem of unemployed soldiers by creating a permanent standing army—the first to exist in western Europe since the days of the Roman Empire.

    C. Kings relied on infantry so heavily because foot soldiers became increasingly effective against knights during the Hundred Years

War, thanks to the adoption of a new missile weapon, the longbow.

1. Before the Hundred Years War, the most common missile weapons were short bows, which were hampered by an inability to punch through armor, and crossbows, which were hampered by a slow rate of fire.
2. The longbow combined the power of the crossbow and the speed of the short bow.
3. The longbow seems to have been developed first in Wales. In the 13th century, the English encountered this weapon during their wars against the Welsh, then used it, in turn, against the French at the Battles of Crécy, Poitiers, and Agincourt.

Suggested Readings:

Ann Astell and Bonnie Wheeler, eds., *Joan of Arc and Spirituality*.

Régine Pernoud and Marie-Véronique Clin, *Joan of Arc: Her Story*.

Michael Prestwich, *Armies and Warfare in the Middle Ages: The English Experience*.

Bonnie Wheeler, ed., *Fresh Verdicts on Joan of Arc*.

Questions to Consider:

1. To what extent did the outcome of the Hundred Years War justify France's and England's expenditures of effort during the war?
2. Have there been other cases in European history where protracted warfare resulted in the emergence of more powerful central government? Is it the case that war naturally tends to increase the power of central governments?

Lecture Seven
The Black Death, Part 1

Scope: The Black Death struck Europe between 1347 and 1351, but even before 1347, Europe was experiencing severe demographic difficulties. Its population had reached an upper limit that was difficult to sustain. With the coming of the Black Death—most likely bubonic plague, operating in conjunction with pneumonic and septicaemic plague—Europe's population began to drop precipitously, and recurrences of the Black Death caused further drops. Contemporaries reacted to the plague in a variety of ways, such as the flagellant movement; although perhaps bizarre to modern observers, these reactions reflected the medical and cultural assumptions of the period. None of these responses warded off the disease effectively. The population of Europe dropped by at least one-third and quite possibly by as much as one-half during the initial outbreak; the population remained at a low level and even continued to drop until the second half of the 15th century, at which point it began to rise again.

Outline

I. After three centuries of demographic expansion during the High Middle Ages, by 1300, Europe was showing signs of overpopulation.

   A. To produce the food needed to sustain its people, Europeans brought marginal land under cultivation.

   B. The Great Famine of 1315, which struck northern Europe, was the worst famine in centuries, killing perhaps 5 to 10 percent of the population in affected areas.

   C. Food shortages were a notable problem in southern Europe in the 1330s and 1340s, forcing towns to hijack grain shipments headed elsewhere.

II. Famine and food shortages may well have paved the way for the Black Death by making Europeans more susceptible to disease. The precise identification of the Black Death, though, has been controversial.

A. The term *Black Death* was coined in the 16th and 17th centuries—contemporaries spoke of the *Great Mortality*, focusing on the number of victims, rather than on the symptoms.

B. The culprit most commonly identified as the Black Death is plague; although this identification is challenged periodically, it is still widely accepted.

  1. Plague is caused by the *Yersinia pestis* bacterium, which is native to central Asia and East Africa and ordinarily resides innocuously in the digestive tracts of fleas, especially rat fleas.

  2. On occasion, the bacteria multiply to the point at which the flea passes the bacteria to the host on which it feeds, infecting and, more often than not, killing the host. As the normal hosts die, rat fleas look to feed on other mammals, including humans.

  3. Bubonic plague, the most common strain of plague, is characterized by the development of a black pustule, or *bubo*, at the point of the bite and elsewhere. Most often, the victim dies within a week.

  4. Pneumonic plague is transmitted not by fleas but from victim to victim—the *Y. pestis* bacteria travel in the bloody phlegm coughed up by their victims. Pneumonic plague kills nearly all its victims.

  5. Septicaemic plague, like bubonic plague, is transmitted to humans by fleas, but it is much faster and more lethal than bubonic plague, killing nearly all its victims within a day, even before pustules can form.

C. The rat flea is hardy and prefers warm and humid conditions. Its preferences would help to explain the seasonal variations of the Black Death, which became active in the spring, reached its peak in late summer and early autumn, and became inactive in the winter.

III. The Black Death was not solely a European phenomenon. It originated elsewhere, and the pattern of its spread in Europe reflects the nature of the medieval European commercial economy.

A. The 14th-century eruption of plague appears to have started in Asia, most likely in Mongolia, some 15 to 20 years before the disease reached Europe.

B. Even before 1347, Europeans had heard rumors of a pestilence killing unprecedented numbers of people to the east.

C. After reaching Egypt and Constantinople in 1347, the Black Death made its way to Sicily and southern Italy, apparently on an Italian trading vessel, late in 1347.

D. Having established a foothold in western Europe, the Black Death struck Europe in full force in the spring of 1348, following existing commercial networks. Mediterranean Europe, nearly all of France, and southern England were affected by the end of 1348; Germany and nearly the whole of the British Isles, by the end of 1349; Scandinavia and eastern Europe, by the end of 1350; and Russia, by the end of 1351, at which point the Black Death vanished across Europe.

IV. Contemporaries most often sought to explain the Black Death in theological or astrological terms, and the remedies they devised reflected those explanations.

    A. Many interpreted the Black Death as divine punishment for human sins; as such, it could be warded off only through penance for those sins.

    B. The flagellant movement that spread during the time of the Black Death represented one such penitential response.

        1. Flagellants were individuals who whipped themselves in violent public processions.

        2. Secular and ecclesiastical authorities were suspicious of flagellants, who were lay people that sometimes claimed priestly powers for themselves and attacked those—Christian clerics and, perhaps, Jews—whose failings had brought about divine punishment.

    C. Another popular explanation for the Black Death was astrological: A conjunction of the planets had polluted the Earth's atmosphere.

    D. Some argued that the Black Death had been caused by Europe's Jews, who had supposedly poisoned Christians in an attempt to wipe them out.

        1. These accusations helped to fuel pogroms, which broke out in Spain, southern France, Switzerland, and Germany.

        2. Popes, kings, and local leaders tended to condemn these pogroms and the disorder they caused, although these condemnations came too late to prevent the attacks and similar ones against lepers.

V. The standard figure given for the Black Death's mortality rate is one in three—that is, between 1347 and 1351, one-third of Europe's people died. This figure should be regarded as a minimum, though; detailed local research has led some historians to conclude that a more accurate mortality rate would be about one in two, with lower mortality rates in northern Europe and even higher ones in Mediterranean Europe.

Suggested Readings:

John Aberth, ed., *The Black Death. The Great Mortality of 1348–1350: A Brief History with Documents.*

Ole Benedictow, *The Black Death, 1346–1353: The Complete History.*

William Jordan, *The Great Famine: Northern Europe in the Early Fourteenth Century.*

Elizabeth A. Lehfeldt, ed., *The Black Death.*

Questions to Consider:

1. What historical events, if any, can compare in scope and magnitude to the Black Death?

2. If the United States were to lose one-third to one-half of its population in a four-year span, what would life be like afterward?

Lecture Eight
The Black Death, Part 2

Scope: The loss of somewhere between one-third and one-half of its population during the space of four years was bound to have profound cultural, social, and economic consequences for late-medieval Europe. Those consequences were magnified by subsequent reappearances of the Black Death—until the second half of the 15th century, regional and continental outbreaks occurred, on average, at least once a decade. Those who survived the Black Death regarded that event as a shattering one that transformed their lives forever, yet at no point did medieval European society fail to function, even if massive depopulation impaired that functioning. Socially, the Black Death increased geographical mobility, drove wages up, drove rents and land values down, and (despite extreme fluctuations from year to year) generally drove food prices down. As a result, in general, the poor got richer and the rich got poorer. That trend, in turn, generated social tensions that sometimes manifested themselves in revolt.

Outline

I. Those who witnessed the Black Death regarded it as the fundamental dividing line in their lives—afterward, they would speak of the time before and the time after the Great Mortality as constituting two different eras.

   A. Petrarch, for example, noting how empty and quiet the world seemed afterward, doubted that subsequent generations would believe his description of Europe as it existed after the Black Death. More obscure authors without Petrarch's literary ambitions wrote similarly.

   B. Boccaccio, in the *Decameron* (written between 1349 and 1351), provided the most famous description of how life was lived during the Black Death. He emphasized the variety of responses, ranging from self-incarceration, to licentiousness, to carrying on as best as one could.

C. The Black Death shocked contemporaries and interfered with the functioning of society at many levels, but this interference never resulted in a complete breakdown.

II. Although the Black Death of 1347 to 1351 was of the greatest psychological consequence, subsequent outbreaks (the first came in 1361) were just as demographically important, driving the European population lower still.

    A. Depopulation affected both town and countryside.

        1. The population of the city of Florence dropped from 120,000 in 1338 to 38,000 in 1427.

        2. Thousands of villages were abandoned entirely in the Late Middle Ages, probably because the Black Death had reduced their populations to unsustainably low levels.

    B. Europe's population in 1450 was probably 60 percent lower than it had been in 1300, and it may not have reached the level of 1300 again until 1600.

III. Depopulation was economically beneficial to some Europeans and economically disastrous for others.

    A. After the Black Death, vacant land was readily available and labor was scarce. As a result, wages shot up (often tripling or quadrupling within a few years of the Black Death's arrival), while land values plummeted, rents dropped, and food prices generally dropped.

    B. These trends favored the poor, whose purchasing power increased markedly. Those who were wealthy found themselves at a relative disadvantage.

    C. The economic consequences of the Black Death could be more complicated than that, though. Artisans who worked in trades that produced for the mass market—clothworkers, for example—were hurt by depopulation, while artisans who worked in luxury trades (such as goldsmiths) benefited from the increase in per capita wealth.

    D. Landowners and other employers reacted to this unfavorable economic situation in a number of different, even contradictory, ways.

        1. One reaction was to try to restore the pre-plague economy by turning back the clock. England's Statute of Labourers, enacted in 1351, attempted to freeze wages at pre-plague levels. Similar laws, passed in other kingdoms and in individual towns and cities, did not prevent rising wages but were nettlesome to those prosecuted for accepting such wages.

    2. Some estate owners attempted to revive serfdom, which would give them access to unpaid labor and prevent peasant movement. Attempts to impose serfdom on peasants generally succeeded in eastern Europe (where serfdom had been rare before) but failed in western Europe, largely thanks to peasant resistance and limited royal support.

IV. Scholars are divided over the issue of whether a morbid and macabre fascination with death became one of the defining characteristics of late-medieval culture.

    A. On the one hand, there does seem to be a keener awareness of the imminence and randomness of death in the decades following the Black Death.

        1. The Dance of Death, in which the figure of Death leads away people of different ages, sexes, and stations, first appears as a motif in poetry and art during the second half of the 14th century and the first half of the 15th century.

        2. *Transi tombs* depicted the deceased in a grotesque state of decay. They first were used in the late 14th century and achieved a certain level of popularity in the 15th century.

    B. On the other hand, scholars have pointed out that the *memento mori*, or "memento of death," had existed before the Late Middle Ages and that the theological message of the transi tomb was no different than the message conveyed by the more serene funerary monuments of the High Middle Ages.

Suggested Readings:

Kathleen Cohen, *Metamorphosis of a Death Symbol: The Transi Tomb in the Late Middle Ages*.

Harry Miskimin, *The Economy of Early Renaissance Europe, 1300–1460*.

William Naphy and Andrew Spicer, *Plague: Black Death and Pestilence in Europe*.

Questions to Consider:

1. It has been suggested that the economic conditions of the post-plague period made it the golden age of workers. In what other periods, if any, have laborers enjoyed a similar rise in their standards of living?

2. If a medieval historian was trying to assess the psychological consequences of the Black Death for survivors, what would be the best way for that historian to go about it? Can historians ever hope to address a topic such as past psychology with the same certitude as, say, past politics?

Lecture Nine
Revolt in Town and Country

Scope: Compared to the Early and the High Middle Ages, the Late Middle Ages witnessed a relatively high number of large-scale revolts, in both rural and urban areas. Taking as our examples the English Peasants Revolt of 1381 and the revolt of the *Ciompi* in Florence in 1378, we can see how peasant uprisings responded to post-plague social tensions as well as to political and military events, such as defeats in the Hundred Years War and the increasing frequency of direct royal taxation. Urban revolts, too, reflected post-plague economic conditions, which exacerbated tensions between merchants and artisans, on the one hand, and among master artisans, journeymen, and apprentices, on the other. Although both the English Peasants Revolt and the revolt of the *Ciompi* were suppressed, these revolts and others like them kept contemporaries on edge.

Outline

I. The English Peasants Revolt of 1381 arose from a conjunction of political and military events, on the one hand, and the challenges of the post-plague economy, on the other hand.

    A. Peasants resented the Statute of Labourers (1351), which tried to return wages to pre-plague levels, and attempts by lords to enforce more strictly and to spread the burdens of serfdom.

    B. By 1380, French raids along England's coast had made local populations fearful and resentful of royal taxes, collected for a war that was no longer going England's way. Indeed, the proximate cause for the English Peasants Revolt of 1381 was a series of direct royal taxes collected in 1377, 1379, and 1380.

II. The English Peasants Revolt lasted only one summer, but the impression it made on contemporaries was much greater than its duration suggests.

    A. At the end of May 1381, peasants in southeastern England attacked royal tax collectors. Within days, there was a wave of similar uprisings in the region as peasants attacked both royal tax collectors and officials and noble estates and monasteries.

B. On June 13, the peasants entered London itself, where they killed royal officials and destroyed government records.

C. Although the peasants attacked royal officials, they distinguished between the king and his government—their avowed intention was to rescue the king from his advisors, whom they blamed for the royal policies of which they disapproved.

III. By the second week of June, leaders had emerged among the peasant rebels: Wat Tyler and John Ball, a renegade priest whose ideas appealed to some among the peasants.

A. Since the 1360s, John Ball had been in prison, locked up on account of his subversive preaching. After the peasants released Ball, he preached to them charged sermons advocating the abolition of all social distinctions based on wealth and birth.

B. John Ball also wanted the upper levels of the English church hierarchy to be abolished, monasteries to be dissolved, and church property to be confiscated and distributed to the laity.

C. On June 13 and 14, King Richard II of England met with the rebel leaders and indicated his willingness to accept some of their demands, such as the abolition of serfdom in certain parts of England.

D. On June 15, when Wat Tyler issued a set of new demands, he was seized and killed by some of the king's companions. The peasant revolt then fell apart; throughout the rest of the summer, nobles and royal officials rounded up remaining rebels and executed many of them.

IV. Perhaps the most famous urban revolt of the Late Middle Ages is the revolt of the *Ciompi* in Florence in 1378. Like the English Peasants Revolt, the revolt of the *Ciompi* reflected both general post-plague conditions and local peculiarities.

A. In post-plague towns, relations between wealthy merchants and financiers, on the one hand, and artisans (skilled craftsman), on the other, were often strained. Artisans adversely affected by depopulation found themselves forced to take employment from merchants, with a corresponding loss of economic independence.

B. Merchants also gained at the expense of urban craftsman by relying more heavily on the *putting-out system*, which allowed merchants to obtain their wares from unregulated rural manufacturers instead of from urban manufacturers subject to guild regulation.

C. Relations within individual trades were likewise strained as master craftsmen, in order to eliminate competition and overproduction, made it more difficult for apprentices and journeymen to become masters.

    1. Masters lengthened the amount of time one had to spend as an apprentice and a journeyman.

    2. Masters raised the fee aspiring masters had to pay to their guild.

    3. Masters made it more difficult for candidates to complete and submit the "masterpiece" that gained one the status of master.

V. In Florence in 1378, clothworkers, including the *Ciompi* (unskilled wage laborers), seized control of the town government for a number of years.

    A. The cloth industry was organized peculiarly in Florence. A single guild, the *Arte della Lana*, governed all clothworkers, but only merchant-cloth manufacturers were members of the guild. Dyers, fullers, weavers, carders, and the like were forbidden to have their own guilds.

    B. In 1378, after clothworkers became involved in a struggle among the city's ruling elite, the *Ciompi* and other clothworkers seized control of Florence and appointed a wool carder as the head of the city's new government.

    C. In power, the *Ciompi* created guilds for the various trades involved in the cloth industry, granted full citizenship to clothworkers, and forbade imprisonment for non-payment of debts.

    D. By August 1378, fights had broken out among various groups of clothworkers, and by 1382, the revolutionary government had fallen.

    E. The aftermath of the *Ciompi* revolt was relatively bloodless compared to the aftermath of the English Peasants Revolt and similar peasant revolts, which suggests that contemporaries were more fearful of rural unrest than of urban unrest.

Suggested Readings:

Samuel Kline Cohn, *The Laboring Classes in Renaissance Florence.*

Guy Fourquin, *The Anatomy of Popular Rebellion in the Middle Ages.*

Rodney Hilton, *Bond Men Made Free: Medieval Peasant Movements and the English Rising of 1381.*

Michel Mollat and Philippe Wolff, *The Popular Revolutions of the Late Middle Ages.*

Questions to Consider:

1. Some, though not all, of the scholarship on late-medieval revolt is informed by the ideas of Karl Marx. What is the proper place of Marxist thought and of modern social theories in general in medieval scholarship? Why do some historians employ social theory in their work, and why do others decline to do so?

2. Does the greater rebelliousness of the Late Middle Ages reflect an illusion generated by the greater amount of source material available for that period, as compared to the High and Early Middle Ages? Can historians ever control for the fact that the amount and the types of evidence available to them change over time, and if so, how?

Lecture Ten
William Ockham

Scope: Although the rise of Humanism—to be discussed in a later lecture—is perhaps the most important development in late-medieval intellectual history, Scholastic theologians also produced works that were significant and controversial. William Ockham was one such theologian. An Englishman and a member of the Franciscan Order until his death in 1349, Ockham's views on the relationship between God and the created world, as well as his views on how human beings achieve salvation, differed somewhat from those espoused by his 13th-century predecessors, such as Thomas Aquinas. Ockham was also involved in disputes concerning the development of his own Franciscan Order, and this involvement, in turn, led him to break with, and become a vocal critic of, the papacy. He also became an early advocate of a mild version of conciliarism. His theological views and criticisms of the papacy made Ockham a polarizing figure during his lifetime and for centuries to come.

Outline

I. Until his late 30s, William Ockham spent his entire life in England, and his career was no different from that of many other contemporary theologians.

   A. Ockham was most likely born in the mid- to late 1280s, and he entered the Franciscan Order before the age of 14.

   B. He studied at Oxford University in the 1310s and early 1320s, receiving the standard training given to Scholastic thinkers, with an emphasis on the study of formal logic and Aristotle. He began writing philosophical treatises and, perhaps, theological ones during this time.

       1. *Scholasticism* refers to a method of teaching, writing, and thinking that had emerged in urban European schools during the 12th and 13th centuries.

       2. Scholastics sought to establish truth by posing questions, by juxtaposing the different answers given to the question at hand by the most respected textual authorities (for example, the

Bible; the writings of church fathers, such as Saint Augustine; and the writings of ancient Roman and Greek philosophers), and by resolving the apparent contradictions among these authorities through philological analysis and the rules of formal logic.

    C. In 1324, Ockham traveled to Avignon, where his writings were examined for heresy. Although no formal condemnation came from this examination, Ockham never again returned to England.

II. Although Ockham was a typical medieval thinker in his mixing of philosophy and theology, which he would have regarded as inseparable, his views on specific subjects caused some of his contemporaries to regard him as potentially a heretic.

    A. Although Ockham, like other medieval thinkers, understood the difference between philosophy (whose object is the created world) and theology (whose object is God and God's revelation), he was comfortable raising theological issues in ostensibly philosophical works (and vice versa).

    B. Central to Ockham's theology is the notion that God is the only necessary being and that there exists an enormous difference between the all-powerful God who creates, on the one hand, and the created world, on the other.

    C. Although these premises were commonplace, the conclusions that Ockham drew from them were challenging, as is evident in Ockham's critique of natural theology.

        1. Thomas Aquinas, Ockham's 13th-century predecessor, had confidence in the field of natural theology. Aquinas believed that it was possible to learn about the nature of God by observing the natural world that God had created. Indeed, Aquinas constructed proofs of God's existence that took observation of natural phenomenon (movement, for example) as their starting points.

        2. Ockham was far less confident about the field of natural theology. He pointed out that God, being all-powerful, might have created the world in an infinite number of different ways, wholly unlike any that we can imagine. If that is the case, how can human beings deduce anything about God's nature from just one of an infinite number of different worlds? The only way to know about God was through Scripture.

3. For Ockham, to suggest that this world reflected the nature of God was to deny divine omnipotence, because it implied that God could not have created the world differently. To say that God forbade murder, theft, and the like because they are inherently bad and God is good is to limit God's freedom of action and to deny divine omnipotence. Rather, murder and theft are bad because God had forbidden them. God might just as easily have deemed murder to be a moral good.

4. Ockham's critics accused him of depicting God as arbitrary.

D. Ockham extended his critique to the sacramental system and *soteriology* (the doctrine of salvation).

    1. Both Aquinas and Ockham agreed that good works and the sacramental system were necessary for salvation and that predestination should be understood as God's foreknowledge of our freely taken actions.

    2. Aquinas posited that, temporally, divine grace, made available to humanity through the sacraments, came first. The believer was free to accept or reject this grace—if accepted, the believer could then do good works and achieve salvation.

    3. Ockham maintained that good works came first and grace came afterward. He made this distinction because it seemed to him to preserve divine freedom best—God freely responded to each human being's actions rather than automatically dispensing grace—but Ockham's assertion left him open to the charge of downplaying or denying the role of grace in salvation.

III. Ockham stayed at Avignon from 1324 to 1328, at which point, he fled to the court of the Holy Roman Emperor, who sheltered Ockham and permitted him to live in Munich until his death. The issue that precipitated Ockham's flight from Avignon and his subsequent attacks on the papacy was the poverty controversy that roiled the Franciscan Order during the 13th and 14th centuries.

A. When Francis of Assisi founded the Franciscan Order in the early 13th century, he established poverty as one of the order's hallmarks. The Franciscans, individually and collectively, were forbidden to own property.

B. As the Franciscan Order grew, it became increasingly difficult to maintain this strict observance of the rules regarding poverty, and the Franciscan Order split into rival groups: the Conventuals, who constituted the majority and believed that rules regarding poverty had to be changed to reflect the changing situation, and the Spirituals, who regarded any failure to adhere to the rules drawn up by Francis of Assisi as reprehensible.

C. In 1322 and 1323, Pope John XXII abrogated an earlier papal bull and ruled that Franciscans could own property. He also ruled that those who maintained that Jesus and his apostles had owned no property were in error.

D. Ockham was affiliated with the Spiritual camp, and he broke with the papacy over John XXII's ruling.

E. After 1328, Ockham never again wrote about theological or philosophical subjects and, instead, devoted himself to writing about the nature of papal power and the steps that could be taken when a pope fell into heresy, as Ockham maintained John XXII had done.

Suggested Readings:

David Burr, *The Spiritual Franciscans: From Persecution to Protest in the Century after Saint Francis.*

Steven Ozment, *The Age of Reform, 1250–1550.*

Paul Vincent Spade, *The Cambridge Companion to Ockham.*

Questions to Consider:

1. If you had been a Franciscan in the early 14th century, would you have sided with the Conventuals or the Spirituals? Why?

2. What are the advantages and disadvantages of the biographical approach to history?

Lecture Eleven
John Wycliffe and the Lollards

Scope: Like William Ockham, John Wycliffe was a controversial English
Scholastic theologian whose ideas concerning the church,
priesthood, and spiritual authority landed him in considerable
trouble. If anything, though, Wycliffe's immediate impact was
even greater, because Wycliffe belonged to a later generation.
Born (most likely) in the 1320s, Wycliffe's work achieved renown
during the troubled 1370s, in the context of the Great Papal
Schism and the English Peasants Revolt of 1381, which made
contemporary authorities that much more suspicious of Wycliffe's
apparent subversiveness. In a sense, their suspicion was not
unfounded, because Wycliffe, unlike Ockham, became the
inspiration for a large-scale heretical movement, Lollardy, the first
such movement to emerge in medieval England.

Outline

I. Late-medieval heretical movements, though arising from the same
forces that spawned similar movements in the High Middle Ages,
nonetheless had distinctive characteristics that set them apart from their
predecessors.

   A. Heresy (an error in religious practice or belief) emerged as a result
   of popular discontent with clerical morals, as well as rising rates of
   lay literacy that encouraged individual reading and interpretation
   of the Bible.

   B. Whereas the biggest heretical movements of the High Middle Ages
   were in Mediterranean Europe and the Low Countries, the mass
   movements of the Late Middle Ages emerged in northern Europe
   (England) and central Europe (Bohemia).

   C. High heresy (heretical ideas espoused by leading theologians) and
   popular heresy remained distinct and unconnected in the High
   Middle Ages, but the two fused in the Late Middle Ages as
   university professors, such as John Wycliffe and Jan Hus, acquired
   large followings.

D. High-medieval heretical movements tended to be nonviolent (the Waldensians were pacifists and the Cathars fought largely in self-defense), but late-medieval heresies (especially the Hussite movement) tended toward militancy.

II. Like Ockham before him, John Wycliffe was a university professor whose career was disrupted as a result of his writings and the suspicions of heterodoxy they raised.

    A. Wycliffe was born most likely in the 1320s and ordained as a priest in 1351; he then went to Oxford to study, remaining there for nearly the rest of his life.

    B. In the early 1370s, Wycliffe took a doctorate in theology and became an important official in the royal administration, which allowed him to establish connections to the English royal family.

    C. In 1377, royal officials protected Wycliffe when the archbishop of Canterbury questioned him about his religious orthodoxy. Although the archbishop issued no condemnation afterward, in that same year, Pope Gregory XI formally condemned 19 articles drawn from Wycliffe's treatise *On Civil Lordship*, written the previous year.

    D. Despite this condemnation, Wycliffe remained at Oxford for several more years, publishing *On the Church* (1378) and *On the Eucharist* (1379), works that were just as controversial as *On Civil Lordship*.

    E. Wycliffe was blamed, almost certainly without cause, for contributing to the English Peasants Revolt of 1381.

        1. Although the ideas of John Ball resembled Wycliffe's ideas, Ball had been thrown in prison for espousing such ideas long before Wycliffe's writings became controversial.

        2. Following the English Peasants Revolt, Wycliffe left Oxford University in 1381.

    F. Although he died of natural causes in 1384, the Council of Constance condemned Wycliffe as a heretic in 1415, and in 1428, his remains were exhumed, burned, and scattered.

III. Wycliffe's ideas, like those of every thinker, changed over time, but he became associated with a few specific positions and arguments.

A. Wycliffe argued that those in a state of mortal sin were unworthy of serving as priests or bishops or holding secular office. In practice, Wycliffe robbed this idea of any revolutionary implication by maintaining that human beings could never truly know whether a secular or ecclesiastical official was in a state of mortal sin; therefore, no one had the right to refuse obedience on those grounds.

B. Wycliffe identified the Bible as the supreme source of religious authority, and although scholars disagree as to whether Wycliffe went so far as to make the Bible the exclusive source of spiritual authority, certainly that is what some of his followers understood him to say. Wycliffe rejected institutions and practices that, in his opinion, had no scriptural justification.

C. Wycliffe blamed the church's wealth for causing moral failings among the clergy, and he advocated the seizure and redistribution of any church wealth beyond the minimum needed to function.

D. To contemporaries, Wycliffe's teachings about the Eucharist were the most consternating. Wycliffe rejected the doctrine of transubstantiation, which explained how bread and wine became the body and blood of Christ during the Mass.

E. For Wycliffe and his followers, the Bible was uniquely important for determining the validity of all religious beliefs and practices; thus, Wycliffe's followers made the Bible more readily available to the laity by undertaking the first translations of the Bible into English.

F. Wycliffe never achieved the notoriety or influence of later thinkers whose ideas in some respects resembled his, such as Martin Luther.
   1. Wycliffe did not have a theory of salvation to equal Luther's doctrine of justification by faith.
   2. The political fragmentation of Germany was conducive to the persistence of Luther's ideas, which also spread quickly thanks to the development of the printing press c. 1450.

G. Nonetheless, Wycliffe did acquire a mass following among the Lollards.

IV. Wycliffe showed some interest in spreading his ideas beyond academic circles, but the creation of Lollardy was the work of his immediate followers rather than of Wycliffe himself.

    A. Wycliffe preached public sermons, and he may have published treatises in the vernacular.

    B. Even before Wycliffe's death, contemporaries referred to individuals who adhered to ideas associated with Wycliffe as *Lollards*, a term of uncertain etymology that might have meant "mumbler" and referred to Lollard Bible reading.

    C. Before the emergence of the Lollards, England had been remarkably free of heretical movements. No full-time inquisitors had been created there in the High Middle Ages, which made it difficult for officials to deal with Lollardy.

    D. Lollardy lacked the distinctive rituals and beliefs of other heretical groups—what defined them was their practice of secret group Bible reading.

    E. Although Wycliffe and the earliest Lollards tended toward pacifism, the movement became more militant in the face of prosecution. Indeed, the Lollards launched two revolts, first in 1414 (Oldcastle's Revolt), then again in 1431. Neither revolt rivaled the English Peasants Revolt of 1381 in size or intensity, but both served to confirm official fears of Lollardy, which nonetheless survived into the Reformation period.

Suggested Readings:

Anne Hudson, *The Premature Reformation: Wycliffite Texts and Lollard History.*

Anthony Kenny, *Wyclif.*

Malcolm Lambert, *Medieval Heresy: Popular Movements from the Gregorian Reform to the Reformation*, 3rd ed.

Shannon McSheffrey, *Gender and Heresy: Women and Men in Lollard Communities, 1420–1530.*

Questions to Consider:

1. How indebted were Martin Luther and the Protestant Reformation to John Wycliffe?

2. There is a gap between those of Wycliffe's ideas that modern students find most interesting and challenging and those that his contemporaries found most interesting and challenging. Why is that? Can you think of examples of individuals who were famous in their own day and again centuries later but for different reasons?

Lecture Twelve
Jan Hus and the Hussite Rebellion

Scope: John Wycliffe's influence extended beyond England—it was especially strong in Bohemia (located in the present-day Czech Republic), where his ideas proved attractive to many Czechs, including a professor at the University of Prague named Jan Hus. Although Hus was not as original a thinker as Wycliffe, he nonetheless became a powerful and popular defender of Wycliffe's ideas against German officials and professors, who sought to stamp out the teaching of Wycliffe in Bohemia. Hus, having sought a guarantee of safe conduct from the Holy Roman Emperor Sigismund, traveled to the Council of Constance to defend his views. At the council he was arrested, tried for heresy, convicted, and executed in 1415. The execution of Hus—especially the manner in which he had been apprehended and tried—touched off a series of revolts known as the Hussite Wars, during which the Hussites became the only medieval heretical group to fight successfully for the establishment of their own church.

Outline

I. Jan Hus's education and early career centered on the University of Prague, where he became a figure of local, then national, importance.

  A. He was born c. 1372 and enrolled at the University of Prague around 1390.

  B. His ambition was to become a priest, which he thought would be easier than working as a peasant, and he was ordained as a priest around 1400.

  C. In 1402, Hus was named as preacher at the Bethlehem Chapel at the University of Prague, which enabled him to make and maintain contact with a non-academic audience. In 1409, Hus became rector of the university itself.

  D. Bohemia, although Czech-speaking, was part of the Holy Roman Empire, which centered on the Kingdom of Germany. At the University of Prague and in Bohemia more generally, Germans held the best and most desirable positions, a fact that was much resented by the local Czech population.

    E. As Czech students became aware of Wycliffe's writings, they embraced his ideas, while Germans feared the disruption that Wycliffe's ideas might cause. Hus became one of the Czechs who openly praised Wycliffe.

II. Tensions between Germans and Czechs over Wycliffe's writings resulted in attempts by German authorities to ban access to Wycliffe and Czech attempts to defy that ban. During the course of this struggle, Hus became more broadly critical of existing ecclesiastical institutions.

    A. In 1409, after the archbishop of Prague, with the support of the pope at Pisa, attempted to seize all of Wycliffe's writings circulating in Prague and to keep Hus from preaching, Hus denounced the archbishop and was excommunicated, drawing international attention in the process.

    B. In 1411, Hus publicly denied the power of popes to issue crusading indulgences and expressed doubts about the existence of purgatory, leading to public demonstrations against crusade preachers and a second excommunication for Hus.

    C. In 1412, Hus left Prague and began to travel throughout Bohemia, where he preached and wrote his most significant work, *Concerning the Church*, which reflects the strong influence of Wycliffe on his thinking.

III. In 1414, Hus traveled to the Council of Constance to explain his views. There, he was arrested, tried and convicted of heresy, and executed.

    A. The Holy Roman Emperor Sigismund engineered the summoning of the Council of Constance primarily because he hoped it would end the Great Papal Schism, but he also wanted it to address the problem of Jan Hus.

    B. Sigismund and the king of Bohemia, Wenceslas, asked Hus to attend the Council and to defend his views there. After Sigismund offered Hus a guarantee of safe conduct, Hus agreed to go.

    C. At the Council, Hus was arrested and charged with accepting certain of Wycliffe's ideas that had been condemned as heretical. Hus admitted that he accepted some of those statements but maintained that they were not heretical if properly understood.

D. In July 1415, the Council formally condemned Hus as a heretic and, after Hus once again refused to recant, handed him over to secular authorities to be burned at the stake.

IV. The death of Hus touched off an armed revolt by Hus's followers who, despite the divisions that emerged among them, managed to fend off all attempts to stamp them out. Their victories allowed them to establish in Bohemia an independent Hussite church, which persisted into the 17th century.

    A. Even while Hus's trial at the Council of Constance was ongoing, Hus's supporters in Bohemia had rallied behind him and protested his treatment.

    B. Perhaps the most distinctive demand made by the Bohemian Hussites was that they be allowed to receive both the consecrated bread and wine during the mass, not just the bread—for this reason, Hussites were sometimes known as *Utraquists* (from the Latin word for "both").

    C. After Hus's death, Hussites organized the Hussite League for the purpose of protecting Hussite preachers.

    D. In 1419, following attempts to eliminate Hussite practice, the Hussites in Prague revolted during the *Defenestration of Prague*, touching off a war that pitted the Hussites against the Holy Roman Empire, the papacy, and indeed, the whole of Catholic Europe.

    E. The Hussites themselves split into two camps.

        1. The Utraquists, based in Prague, came to constitute the more moderate group. Their demands generally fell in line with Hus's thinking.

        2. The Taborites, whose strength was in the countryside, were a millenarian group who believed that the end of the world was at hand. They espoused the abolition of private property and an aggressive militancy.

    F. Despite their differences, the two groups formulated a single program, the Four Articles of Prague, issued in 1419, and cooperated in defending themselves against the numerous crusades launched against them thereafter.

    G. After the Hussites had inflicted severe damage on their enemies and after the Utraquists had cooperated with Catholics against the Taborites in 1434, the remaining Hussites, in 1436, secured imperial recognition of a Hussite church that would thereafter coexist with the Catholic Church in Bohemia.

Suggested Readings:

Howard Kaminsky, *A History of the Hussite Revolution*.

Matthew Spinka, *John Hus: A Biography*.

Questions to Consider:

1. Of the three theologians (Ockham, Wycliffe, and Hus) considered here, which one was the most historically important and why?
2. Of all the theological and liturgical issues of the day, why was the Eucharist so often at the center of late-medieval religious debate?

Lecture Thirteen
Witchcraft

Scope: Although the 16th and 17th centuries were the great age of European witch hunts, the first European witch trials date to the Late Middle Ages. A witch was a combination of a heretic and a maleficent magician, granted magical powers in return for entering into a pact with Satan and renouncing Christianity. Although heresy and harmful magic both predated the Late Middle Ages, the two concepts fused between 1300 and 1500 as more individuals came to believe in the existence of witches. Based on the evidence of late-medieval witch trials, it appears that this belief originated in inquisitorial courts, from whence it spread to the rest of society. By 1500, the concept of the witch was well defined, and the stage was set for the explosive growth in the number of witch prosecutions that occurred in the post-Reformation period.

Outline

I. Belief in harmful magic and magicians predated the emergence of Christianity, and heresy had been an issue within Christianity since its formative centuries. It was only between 1300 and 1500, however, that a belief in the existence of a sub-society of heretics who practiced harmful magic—in other words, witches—became commonplace and a sign of religious orthodoxy.

   A. A magical action is one that relies for its effect on mysterious, non-intuitive powers that are manipulated through the performance of specific techniques and rituals.

   B. During the Early and High Middle Ages, there was a popular belief in the existence of magic, which might be used for good or for ill.

   1. Secular authorities were willing to punish severely those who practiced harmful magic, but for the most part, left alone those who practiced beneficial magic.

   2. Some theologians accepted the distinction between good and harmful magic, although others argued that all magic ought to be condemned because it relied on demonic involvement, whether the magician knew it or not.

C. It was difficult to prosecute practitioners of harmful magic, though, because of *talion*, which required accusers who failed to prove their cases to undergo the punishment that the accused would have suffered if convicted. Few accusers were willing to bring a capital charge for a crime that was as hard to prove as harmful magic.

D. Given the risks of talion, the few killings of harmful magicians tended to be carried out by people bypassing the judicial system.

II. During the Late Middle Ages, accusations of, and prosecutions for, the practice of harmful magic increased, and some of those accusations and prosecutions involved a specific type of harmful magic: witchcraft.

A. What distinguished the witch from the ordinary practitioner of harmful magic was the satanic pact. Witches derived their magical powers directly and knowingly from Satan, whom they agreed to worship while abjuring Christianity.

B. Other characteristics came to be associated with witches in the Late Middle Ages. These characteristics included:
  1. The killing and eating of small children.
  2. The use of animal familiars.
  3. The presence of a special mark on witches' bodies.
  4. Membership in an organized sub-society that engaged in night flying and orgiastic devil worship.

C. Beliefs in night flight and the existence of secret societies engaging in orgiastic worship ceremonies predated Christianity; during the High Middle Ages, these activities were associated specifically with heretics. As the concepts of the heretic and the harmful magician came together during the Late Middle Ages, activities associated with heretics came to be associated with witches, as well.

III. One of the most compelling and solidly supported explanations of how and why heresy and harmful magic came together during the Late Middle Ages has been offered by the historian Richard Kieckhefer, whose examination of late-medieval witch trials has identified inquisitorial courts as the milieu in which a belief in the existence of witches first emerged.

A. During the 1230s, medieval inquisitions took on the form for which they are best known today: Instead of relying on local bishops to identify and correct heretics, they instead began to rely on full-time, well-trained inquisitors who imposed penances on heretics who recanted and handed over obdurate or relapsed heretics to secular authorities for execution.

B. Medieval inquisitors collected evidence and testimony on their own initiative—they did not have to wait for specific accusations before bringing charges of heresy, and they were not punished if they failed to prove the charges they brought (a rare enough event, given that they were also the judges).

C. Inquisitorial procedure, therefore, made it easier to prosecute individuals for practicing harmful magic.

D. Initially, inquisitors had no jurisdiction over practitioners of harmful magic, only over heretics. By 1300, inquisitors had acquired that jurisdiction, arguing that all magic was, by definition, a form of heresy because it involved demonic cooperation, whether the magician knew it or not.

E. When inquisitors tried individuals for the practice of harmful magic, they asked the accused all the same questions that they routinely asked of heretics: whether they had engaged in devil worship, whether they met secretly with other heretics, and so on. Those questioned, sometimes under torture, responded yes often enough to convince inquisitors that there existed a substantial number of individuals who practiced harmful magic and devil worship.

F. Belief in witches spread outward from inquisitorial circles via sermons and the public executions of witches, where the specific crimes of the condemned were announced to the audience.

G. The transcripts of late-medieval witch trials, as well as their chronological and geographical spread, lend support to this theory of the rise of witch trials.
   1. Between 1300 and 1375, witch trials were very few in Europe (perhaps one a year), and the accused tended to be powerful and prominent individuals, which suggests that the concept of witchcraft was then circulating only among a small elite.
   2. From 1375 to 1435, the number of witch trials increased, and for the first time, one finds theological works devoted exclusively to witches.

3. From 1435 to 1500, the number of trials continued to increase, and witches were now sometimes accused and executed in batches rather than singly. In 1487, two inquisitors published the most famous and comprehensive late-medieval witch-hunting treatise, the *Malleus maleficarum* (*Hammer of the Witches*).

IV. As accusations of witchcraft became increasingly common, the accused more often were women, especially older, single, and poor women. This pattern persisted in the 16th and 17th centuries.

A. At a popular level, individuals who experienced personal misfortune or disaster sometimes blamed a neighbor for the disaster and accused that neighbor of witchcraft.

B. The neighbor blamed was often someone who had depended on the assistance of others to survive, who had been refused assistance by the person who suffered the misfortune, and who was then accused of bringing about the misfortune as an act of revenge.

C. Because poor, single women over 50 were the ones most often asking for assistance from neighbors, they were the ones most often accused of witchcraft.

D. The authors of the *Malleus maleficarum* lent theoretical support to the association of women and witchcraft, arguing that women resorted to witchcraft in order to compensate for their natural intellectual and moral inferiority.

Suggested Readings:

Hans Peter Broedel, *Malleus Maleficarum and the Construction of Witchcraft: Theology and Popular Belief.*

Richard Kieckhefer, *European Witch Trials: Their Foundations in Popular and Learned Culture, 1300–1500.*

Edward Peters, *The Witch, the Magician, and the Law.*

Questions to Consider:

1. Was it irrational for people to believe in the existence of witches during the Late Middle Ages? If so, do the European witch trials indicate that medieval Europe was a less rational place than modern Europe?

2. Both demography and culture (specifically, ancient beliefs in female inferiority) caused witchcraft to become associated with women. Which of these two factors was the more important in establishing this link? If either one or the other factor had not existed, would witchcraft still have been associated with women more than with men?

Lecture Fourteen
Christine de Pizan and Catherine of Siena

Scope: Of all the late-medieval women to achieve fame for their participation in the era's culture and politics, Christine de Pizan and Catherine of Siena are among the most noteworthy. Christine de Pizan's reputation rested on her writings—she was perhaps the first female author to support herself and her family through her own writing. In such works as *The Book of the City of Ladies* and *The Treasure of the City of Ladies*, Christine de Pizan addressed the issue of female inferiority, thereby helping to launch a literary genre, the *querelle des femmes* ("debate about women"), that continued for centuries. Catherine of Siena's sanctity and asceticism, which struck some contemporaries as extreme, nonetheless made her a central figure in the most important political issues of the day and won her a lasting renown—in 1970, she and the 16th-century mystic Teresa of Avila were the first two women elevated to the status of Doctors of the Church.

Outline

I. Christine de Pizan was famous in her own time for her many writings, some of which dealt with the contentious issue of whether females were morally and intellectually inferior to males.

    A. Such beliefs were as entrenched at the end of the Late Middle Ages as they had been at the beginning.

    B. Authors besides Christine de Pizan, such as Giovanni Boccaccio in his *Concerning Famous Women* and Geoffrey Chaucer in his *Legend of Good Women*, to a certain extent challenged such beliefs by cataloging examples of virtuous women.

    C. During the Late Middle Ages, female authors, too, began to comment on these issues, and the *querelle des femmes* ("debate about women") became a recognizable literary genre, largely thanks to the work of Christine de Pizan and the responses it invited.

II. Because Christine de Pizan inserted autobiographical material into her writings, historians know about her life and career in some detail.

A. Christine was Italian and born around 1365; about her mother we know little, but her father was a physician and astrologer attached to the court of the king of France. He encouraged his daughter to acquire learning beyond what was normal for a girl at that time.

B. Christine married a minor royal official at the age of 15; her relationship with her husband was, like her relationship with her father, good, but both the husband and the father died when Christine was 25, leaving her with the financial responsibility for her family.

C. To support herself and her family, Christine began to write, initially works of poetry but then works of various types (including a treatise on military theory) that would appeal to her aristocratic audience. Her final work, written in 1429 (the year before her death), was an account of Joan of Arc.

D. Christine de Pizan achieved a high degree of popularity in her own day and remained widely published into the early 16th century, at which point she faded into obscurity until scholars drew attention to her once again in the second half of the 20th century.

III. Today, readers are most interested in Christine de Pizan's views on the nature of women and the relationship between the sexes, as discussed in her *Book of the City of Ladies* and *Treasure of the City of Ladies*.

   A. Of these two books, *Treasure of the City of Ladies* was the more conventional and the more popular in its own day. It outlines the duties appropriate to women of different social classes and recommends that women of each social class accept their lot in life.

   B. *Book of the City of Ladies* was influenced by Boccaccio's *Concerning Famous Women* and contains many illustrative examples of virtuous women.

   C. However, *Book of the City of Ladies* also contains its author's argument that male belief in female intellectual inferiority arose from the unequal educational opportunities afforded to women. If women were as educated as men, then it would become apparent to men that females were as capable of learning as males.

   D. The argument that equality in educational opportunity would put an end to belief in female inferiority is one that subsequent female participants in the *querelle des femmes*, and their male allies, took up vigorously.

    E. Christine de Pizan identified other factors that likewise contributed to the belief in female moral inferiority, including a desire on the part of males to flaunt their learning by quoting ancient works of misogynist literature.

IV. Although Christine de Pizan's ability to support herself as an author made her almost one of a kind, Catherine of Siena was one of a number of late-medieval women to achieve fame as mystics and ascetics.

    A. That women achieved fame through mysticism is not surprising— priesthood and the great majority of church offices were forbidden to women, but mystical revelation might come to any believer, male or female, clerical or laic.

    B. Writings played a major role in making Catherine of Siena famous.
        1. During her life, she dictated some 380 letters, which hold an important place in the history of 14th-century Italian literature.
        2. One of her companions, Raymond of Capua, between 1385 and 1395, wrote an admiring and influential account of Catherine of Siena's life and religious practices.

    C. Born perhaps around 1347, Catherine showed signs of her religious vocation at an early age. She clashed with her family over the issue of marriage, which she refused. Instead of marrying, she resided in her family's home in seclusion.

    D. Around the age of 20, she became affiliated with the Dominican Order and began to work among the poor and sick of Siena.

    E. In 1374, the Dominicans appointed Raymond of Capua as her spiritual advisor.

    F. The following year, Catherine received invisible stigmata (marks on the hands and feet believed to correspond to the places where nails had been driven through Jesus of Nazareth).

    G. As a result of her reputation, Catherine became involved in the return of the papacy to Rome, in papal attempts to organize a crusade, and in attempts to end the Great Papal Schism, until her death in 1380.

V. Catherine of Siena became most famous for her great asceticism, as described by Raymond of Capua.

A. From her youth, Catherine practiced self-flagellation and fasting of an especially intense sort, to the point that the only food she would ingest willingly and without vomiting was the Eucharist.

B. Although Catherine of Siena's acts of self-mortification struck some of her contemporaries as too much and strike some modern students as disgusting, those practices were rooted in the theological beliefs and cultural realities of the time.

    1. For all saints, male and female, to suffer was to imitate the sacrifice of Jesus of Nazareth, which had redeemed humanity. Such imitation brought believers closer to God, making them better intercessors for their fellow human beings.

    2. Female saints focused on fasting and Eucharistic practice so much because food was a female concern and something over which they had some control.

Suggested Readings:

Caroline Bynum, *Holy Feast, Holy Fast: The Religious Significance of Food to Medieval Women*.

Thomas Luongo, *The Saintly Politics of Catherine of Siena*.

Karen Scott, "St. Catherine of Siena, 'Apostola.'"

Karen Scott, "Mystical Death, Bodily Death: Catherine of Siena and Raymond of Capua on the Mystic's Encounter with God."

Charity Cannon Willard, *Christine de Pizan: Her Life and Works*.

Questions to Consider:

1. Which is the better source for understanding Catherine of Siena: her dictated letters or Raymond of Capua's account of her life? What should historians do when the two sources differ?

2. What similarities and differences exist between Christine de Pizan and other famous female writers who have addressed the issues of female nature and the relations between the sexes?

Lecture Fifteen
Gunpowder

Scope: The introduction of gunpowder weapons was one of most important technological developments in late-medieval Europe. First found in Europe during the 1320s, cannon became, within a generation or two of their introduction, an indispensable part of the siege of any castle, fortress, or walled town, and at the very end of the Late Middle Ages, individual firearms became, for the first time, an effective weapon that could turn the tide of battle. The development of gunpowder weapons was harmful to those who had most benefited from older technologies and techniques of fighting: knights and nobles, whose body armor could be pierced with relative ease and whose castles could now be reduced to rubble. Acting in conjunction with other developments in military technology, such as the emergence of the pike and the longbow as effective infantry weapons, gunpowder forced the medieval nobility to function less as warriors and more as courtiers.

Outline

I.   At the outset of the Late Middle Ages, even before the appearance of gunpowder weapons, foot soldiers had unexpectedly defeated armies of knights in various parts of Europe, using new weapons and techniques.

    A. In Flanders (1302), Scotland (1314), and Switzerland (1315), foot soldiers defeated knights by developing innovative ways of dealing with cavalry charges, using such weapons as massed pikes or (among the Swiss) halberds.

    B. The Swiss developed tactics that allowed them to use massed pikes offensively as well, making the Swiss the most feared foot soldiers in late-medieval Europe.

II. Recipes for making gunpowder appeared in Europe in the second half of the 13th century, and cannon first came into use in Europe during the 1320s and 1330s, specifically in Italy.

    A. Gunpowder weapons had been used in China for centuries before they came to be used in Europe.

1. Given that cannon first came into use in Italy—still the most important link between Europe and the rest of the world—Asian models were likely important for European development.
2. The Chinese tended to use gunpowder as an explosive, while Europeans used it primarily as a propellant.

B. Cannon in the 1320s and 1330s were inaccurate and dangerous to their users. Initially, they were used largely for their psychological effects on the enemy.

C. Nonetheless, the introduction of cannon revolutionized siege warfare.
   1. Before there were cannon, sieges often lasted for months and sometimes for years, with attackers having to wait until the defenders ran out of supplies. To destroy walls, one had to batter them down or tunnel under them—both were slow and dangerous procedures.
   2. By the 1370s and 1380s, cannon had technically improved to the point at which they were indispensable for any siege, and further improvements were made during the course of the Hundred Years War. For example, stone cannonballs gave way to better cast-iron cannonballs in the 1430s.

D. Firearms did not have the same military impact as cannon in the Late Middle Ages, but by 1500, a primitive type of musket, the *arquebus*, was coming into widespread use. The effectiveness of musketeers against knights was demonstrated at the Battle of Pavia in 1525.

III. Knights and nobles responded to these technological developments by changing the types of armor they wore and the types of castles they built.

A. During the Late Middle Ages, heavy plate armor with sloping surfaces designed to deflect projectiles replaced chain mail as the armor of choice, although the weight and expense of plate armor caused problems of their own.

B. The relatively tall, thin walls of high-medieval castles were good for preventing people from climbing into a castle but ineffective against cannon. During the 14th and 15th centuries, castles and towns made their walls shorter and thicker, with sloping surfaces designed to deflect cannonballs.

C. Although these developments helped to mitigate the effects of gunpowder weapons, they were not able to offset those effects entirely.

IV. The development of gunpowder weapons, together with the unfavorable economic situation facing landowning nobles after the Black Death, forced nobles to adapt in various ways.

    A. Some nobles, attached to their military vocation, joined the standing armies that began to emerge toward the end of the Late Middle Ages.

    B. Many nobles took service in the courts of kings or nobles with greater economic resources than they themselves possessed, becoming courtiers.

    C. In 1528, Baldassare Castiglione published *The Book of the Courtier*, a how-to guide for courtiers that told them what skills they would need to develop if they were to flourish at court.

V. As fighting techniques and the nobility changed, those elements of medieval culture that reflected the knightly ethos dwindled away, but very slowly.

    A. Chivalry, the code of conduct by which knights and other nobles were expected to live, remained a powerful cultural ideal throughout the Late Middle Ages. New chivalric orders were founded in the 14th and 15th centuries.

    B. Jousting, one of the favorite activities of the high-medieval knight, remained common.

    C. By 1500, both chivalry and jousting were on the verge of seeming archaic, although it was not until the 16th and 17th centuries that both finally surrendered the cultural importance they had once enjoyed.

        1. Thomas Malory's *The Death of Arthur*, written in the 15th century, is generally regarded as the last great chivalric romance; the genre subsequently faded away, and when Miguel Cervantes wrote *Don Quixote* in the early 17th century, he regarded chivalry as outdated.

        2. Jousting tournaments died out during the course of the 16th century.

Suggested Readings:

Philippe Contamine, *War in the Middle Ages*.

Jonathan Dewald, *The European Nobility, 1400 to 1800*.

A. G. Dickens, ed., *The Courts of Europe: Politics, Patronage, and Royalty, 1400–1800*.

Maurice Keen, *Chivalry*.

Questions to Consider:

1. What other changes in military technology have equaled or surpassed the emergence of gunpowder weapons in importance?

2. To what extent did medieval chivalry shape European culture after the Middle Ages?

Lecture Sixteen
The Printing Press

Scope: Circa 1450, Johannes Gutenberg invented the printing press. The invention of the printing press was one in a series of developments in medieval Europe that made book production increasingly efficient, yet the printing press was uniquely important among those developments. By combining the use of a press mechanism with movable metal type, Gutenberg and other printers were able to produce books in greater numbers and with greater speed than had ever been possible before, and those books contained fewer production errors than would have been found in handwritten manuscripts. The printing press greatly increased the efficiency with which knowledge was preserved and disseminated, making it easier for subsequent generations to build upon and surpass the intellectual achievements of their predecessors. Less happily, the printing press resulted in a split between spelling and pronunciation that bedevils the English language even today.

Outline

I. The invention of the printing press was a response to growing lay literacy and a corresponding growth in the demand for books. Already during the High Middle Ages, book production had become more efficient in response to growing demand, and books had themselves become more user-friendly.

   A. During the High Middle Ages, paper replaced parchment, which was expensive and difficult to prepare, as the most commonly used writing material.

   B. A new type of handwriting, Gothic script, emerged in high-medieval Europe, which also experienced a revival of cursive writing.
   1. Gothic script was very compact, allowing copyists to fit more words on a single page.
   2. The use of Gothic cursive script allowed copyists to write faster.
   3. Although Gothic script is more efficient than the script that preceded it, namely, Carolingian miniscule, we use

Carolingian miniscule today because Italian Humanists preferred and popularized Carolingian miniscule, which they mistook for a type of ancient Roman handwriting.

    C. Books became more practical during the High Middle Ages, smaller in size and equipped with useful aids such as tables of contents and indexes.

II. Despite these developments, book production remained relatively slow because each page still had to be written by hand. The printing press allowed the mechanical production of books, thereby breaking that bottleneck.

    A. In the late 14th century, some European book producers experimented with producing books using carved blocks of wood or metal plates. Neither of these methods was wholly satisfactory.

        1. The wooden blocks tended to wear out quickly.

        2. Transferring the text from the inked block or plate to the paper was a time-consuming process.

    B. Johannes Gutenberg was a goldsmith who, in the 1430s and 1440s, experimented with new printing techniques in Strasbourg and Mainz. Around 1450, he seems to have developed the first printing press (the oldest extant materials produced by a printing press, presumably Gutenberg's, date to 1454).

        1. Gutenberg replaced the carved wooden block or metal plate with movable metal type that was not only durable but could be arranged and rearranged in an infinite number of ways and with great speed.

        2. Gutenberg also pioneered the use of a pressing mechanism to apply the inked letters to the paper.

    C. By the 1470s, German printers were setting up shop throughout Europe, wherever a significant demand existed for books, and during the 1470s, aspiring printers of various nationalities established their own printing shops. The first English printer was William Caxton, who came across the printing press in Germany and began publishing in England in 1476.

    D. The extent to which Gutenberg's printing press was based on Asian technology has been much discussed.

        1. By the 11th century, Chinese printers were using movable wooden and ceramic type, and in the 13th century, Korean printers used movable metal type.

2. At present, it is neither certain nor out of the question that Gutenberg had somehow learned of these Asian antecedents. The use of the press mechanism, however, was without Asian precedent, and printing quickly assumed a greater importance in Europe than it enjoyed in Asia, in part because the simple European alphabet was especially conducive to printing.

III. The first European printers catered to the tastes of their audience and tried not to revolutionize the nature of the book. Nonetheless, printing was bound to have important cultural and intellectual consequences.

    A. The first European printers tried to make printed books look like handwritten manuscripts by, for example, using illuminations and oversized initial letters, because that is what their customers expected books to look like.

    B. Nonetheless, the printing press changed knowledge.

        1. It made the dissemination of knowledge more rapid.

        2. It made the foundations of knowledge more permanent and secure. Books produced in sufficient numbers were unlikely to disappear forever—they would remain available to all subsequent generations. Printers, like copyists, made errors, but they made fewer errors, and because all the errors in a print run were the same, they could be corrected fairly easily in subsequent editions.

    C. Before printing, spelling was highly variable—the same word might be spelled a dozen different ways. With the advent of printing, as individuals saw certain words spelled the same way repeatedly, spelling became standardized.

        1. The standardization of spelling, on the one hand, made comprehension easier.

        2. On the other hand, even as spelling was frozen, pronunciation continued to change, which explains why today there is a weak relationship between the way English words are spelled and the way they are pronounced (*knight*, *gnat*, and *ghoti* are good examples of this trend).

Suggested Readings:

Elizabeth Eisenstein, *The Printing Press as an Agent of Change*.

Stephen Füssel, *Gutenberg and the Impact of Printing*.

Rudolf Hirsch, *Printing, Selling, and Reading, 1450–1550*, 2nd ed.

Albert Kapr, *Johann Gutenberg: The Man and His Invention*.

Questions to Consider:

1. Which historical development will ultimately prove to be more important: the development of the printing press or the development of the Internet?

2. Which historical development was of greater importance for the Late Middle Ages: gunpowder weapons or the printing press?

Lecture Seventeen
Renaissance Humanism, Part 1

Scope: During the course of the 15th century, certain Italian scholars began to refer to themselves as *Humanists*, and 19th-century scholars subsequently dubbed their educational and intellectual program *Humanism*. Humanist ideas were an essential part of the broader cultural and artistic movement known as the Italian Renaissance. Humanism, as it emerged in 14th-century Italy (specifically Florence), was characterized by: (1) a strong belief in the inherent goodness, the vast intellectual capabilities, and the dignity of humanity and (2) a profound admiration for Classical literature and art and a desire to revive the literary and artistic values of antiquity. In promoting the study of antique literature and the imitation of ancient art, Humanists created new a schema of historical periodization and contributed to the secularization of medieval life—although it is important not to overstate the extent of that secularization.

Outline

I. A number of factors help to explain why Humanism emerged in 14th-century Florence.

   A. Italy had been the most commercially advanced region of Europe during the High Middle Ages. It possessed substantial wealth and relatively high rates of lay literacy; the latter was especially important for a movement whose membership and ethos were relatively secular.

   B. Nowhere else in Europe was the Classical past so physically present and such a matter of national pride as in Italy.

   C. Florence was unusual among important late-medieval towns because it lacked a functioning university. Scholasticism was not as well established in Florence as elsewhere, giving Humanism room to grow there.

   D. At first glance, the troubled 14th and 15th centuries seem like an odd time for the emergence of a cultural movement characterized by boundless optimism and confidence. Economic historians, however, have suggested that the economic conditions of the Black Death contributed to the spread (though not the content) of Humanism: Those who possessed capital were presented with few opportunities to invest their money in financially profitable enterprises and, thus, opted to sink their money into cultural projects instead.

II. During the first three-quarters of the 14th century, Humanism—not yet a self-conscious or self-defined movement—was the work of a few pioneers, whom later Humanists would hail as their inspiration.

    A. In art, Giotto di Bondone (d. 1337) introduced new elements of realism into painting through the use of shading. He lacked any immediate successors, though, and other artists did not follow his lead until the early 15th century.

    B. In letters, Francesco Petrarca, or Petrarch (d. 1374), was the trailblazer.

        1. Petrarch was an ardent student of Classical literature; he rediscovered lost works of Cicero and wrote Latin in flawless imitation of Classical Roman authors.

        2. During the 1330s, Petrarch came to believe that history consisted of three periods: the Classical age, when antique art and letters had flourished, ending with the Sack of Rome in 410; a Middle Age or Dark Age, when art and literature had decayed, persisting into his own lifetime; and a future third age, when Classical art and literature would be reborn.

III. Between roughly 1375 and 1425, Giotto and Petrarch attracted admirers and followers who came to believe that the period of rebirth, for which Petrarch had longed, was at hand. These self-identified Humanists also began to attract the support of patrons.

    A. The chancellor of Florence between 1375 and 1406 was Coluccio Salutati, a Humanist who steered the city's financial resources toward the support of Humanist authors and artists.

    B. Florentine patronage continued through the 15th century, but private patronage became increasingly important as members of the de Medici family used their wealth to finance Humanist scholars and artists.

    C. The de Medici family took an interest in Plato, and the Humanists whom they supported likewise became more interested in Plato and in philosophical issues in general during the second half of the 15th century.

IV. Humanists spoke of themselves as making a complete break with the medieval past. Although they had more in common with their medieval predecessors than they admitted, nonetheless, Humanists were right to believe that there was something new and different about themselves.

    A. Scholastic theologians of the High Middle Ages revered the intellectual authorities of the ancient world, and throughout the Middle Ages, there had been attempts to reform the Latin language and bring it into closer conformity with its Classical usage.

    B. Nonetheless, Humanist admiration for the Classical world was more intense than that of the Scholastics, and as a result, it had unique consequences.

        1. Italian Humanists, following Petrarch, devised a new three-part periodization of all human history (ancient, medieval, modern) that used secular events, such as the sack of Rome, to mark the essential dividing points. This Humanist schema would replace the six-part division of history, based on religious events, associated with Saint Augustine.

        2. Italian Humanists were keenly aware of the cultural gap that existed between their own time and the Classical past, and this recognition helped Humanist scholars and artists to avoid the anachronistic mistakes that their predecessors, who saw themselves and the ancients as more alike than they really were, had been prone to make.

        3. Humanists tended to avoid works of universal history, which had been popular in the Middle Ages (and, in some circles, long afterward). Universal history told the history of the world from the creation to the present, with the purpose of showing divine providence at work throughout. Humanists tended to write works of history that were more limited in scope and geared toward practical political problems. The Humanist approach to history was, in this sense, relatively secular.

    C. As Burckhardt perceived, there was a new emphasis on individualism among Humanists. Humanist artists signed their creations (unlike medieval artists), and Humanist authors saw their work as a means of achieving personal glory and immortality—not as a replacement for Christian immortality but as a supplement to it.

Suggested Readings:

Gene Brucker, *Renaissance Florence*.

Richard Goldthwaite, *Wealth and the Demand for Art in Italy*.

Paul Oskar Kristeller, *Renaissance Thought and Its Sources*.

Questions to Consider:

1. Today, the term *Renaissance* has positive connotations, while the term *medieval* has negative connotations. Are those connotations deserved?

2. To what extent do popular images of the Italian Renaissance today match up to the Renaissance as it existed in the 14th and 15th centuries?

Lecture Eighteen
Renaissance Humanism, Part 2

Scope: In espousing Humanism, the Humanists of the Italian Renaissance were critiquing, implicitly and explicitly, the dominant mode of intellectual inquiry at the time: Scholasticism. With its emphasis on formal logic and its hair-splitting terminological wrangles, Scholasticism (according to its Humanist critics) was of little help in determining the truth. More importantly, with its lack of literary aspiration, Scholasticism failed to bring about moral improvement, and in this respect, Humanists deemed it inferior to Classical literature. Ascribing a moral superiority to pagan literature was controversial, as were some of the specific scholarly projects undertaken by Humanists, such as Lorenzo Valla's scrutiny of the Donation of Constantine and Erasmus's revision of the Bible. Humanist ideas, including the idea that human beings could achieve happiness in this life, had an important place in European intellectual life for centuries to come, in part thanks to the distinctive educational curriculum that Humanists developed and propagated.

Outline

I. Petrarch, in *On His Own Ignorance and That of Many Others*, developed a critique of Scholasticism that other Humanist scholars took up and developed further.

   A. Petrarch doubted that the Scholastic method was capable of determining the truth, and those truths that it did discover were not worth knowing because they were devoid of practical consequences.

   B. For Humanists, Classical literature, thanks to the inspirational beauty of its Latin, was a better instrument of moral guidance and improvement than was Scholastic theology.

   C. In assigning an independent moral value to Classical literature, Humanists opened themselves up to the criticism that they held the pagan authors of antiquity in higher regard than Christian theologians such as Thomas Aquinas.

II. Humanist scholars developed a mastery of Latin and an understanding of philology that allowed them to undertake controversial scholarly projects.

    A. In 1440, the Humanist scholar Lorenzo Valla published a work that challenged the authenticity of the Donation of Constantine.

        1. The Donation of Constantine purported to be a letter from the 4th-century Emperor Constantine to the pope, ceding to him overlordship of the western half of the Roman Empire.

        2. Valla demonstrated that the Latin used in the Donation of Constantine was not the Latin of the 4th century but, rather, the Latin of a later period. Today, most scholars accept that the Donation of Constantine was composed in the 8th century.

        3. Given that the Donation of Constantine had been used to buttress claims of papal superiority vis-à-vis kings and other secular rulers, Valla's analysis was politically significant.

    B. In 1516, the Dutch Humanist Desiderius Erasmus published a new Latin version of the New Testament, revised on the basis of Greek manuscripts.

        1. Erasmus greatly improved his new Latin edition of the Bible in subsequent editions, each time using older Greek versions to suggest how the Latin ought to be emended.

        2. Erasmus's goal was to create a Bible pruned of errors and mistakes, but some contemporaries found his willingness to alter the traditional Latin Vulgate Bible disturbing, because it could be construed as calling into question the extent to which the Bible formed a single, stable, and recoverable text.

III. In the long run, the Humanists' most revolutionary legacy was their revival of a notion that was a commonplace of ancient philosophy but contrary to a dominant strand of Christian thinking: that human beings could attain happiness in this world and ought to work toward achieving that happiness.

    A. In the early 5th century, Saint Augustine, in his *City of God*, had critiqued Classical philosophy precisely because it had sought after human happiness during this lifetime—an unattainable goal, for humans could achieve true happiness only through salvation in the afterlife.

    B. Although Petrarch and other Humanists admired Saint Augustine for the elegance of his Latin prose, they understood human nature rather differently, as rendered only slightly imperfect by original sin and its consequences, rather than devastated by them.

    C. Although all Humanists believed in the existence of a Christian afterlife and desired salvation, they assigned an independent value to doing good in this world—as one Humanist maxim put it, "Man was born to be useful to man."

IV. Humanist ideas spread through society thanks to Humanist schools and the curriculum they taught.

    A. The Humanist educational program, or the *studia humanitatis*, had three main components:

        1. The study of rhetoric, (the art of writing and speaking persuasively), Classical Latin, and Greek literature.

        2. History.

        3. Ethics.

        4. Ethics provided a guide to action, history provided examples of good and bad individuals that reinforced ethical precepts, and rhetoric allowed Humanists to inspire ethical behavior in others.

    B. Because Scholasticism was entrenched in universities, the Humanist curriculum spread more quickly and completely at the level of the secondary school.

    C. Merchants and nobles found Humanist education, with its emphasis on practicality, attractive.

V. In a sense, Renaissance Humanists achieved the opposite of what they intended. Although Humanists hoped to revive Classical values in art and literature and to demonstrate their superiority in relation to medieval art and literature, one unintended consequence of Humanism was to undermine the intellectual authority of the ancient world.

    A. Humanism, like Scholasticism, was fundamentally textual. Old books were considered to be the greatest source of knowledge and wisdom.

    B. Renaissance artists, in trying to achieve a greater naturalism in their work, sponsored dissections of the human body, which in turn, revealed that ancient authors had a flawed understanding of how the human body operated.

C. Although it would take centuries for the implications of this realization to be worked out and applied to other areas of human knowledge, Humanists inadvertently began the process whereby empiricism (direct observation of the natural world) would supplant ancient texts as the ultimate source of intellectual authority in Europe.

Suggested Readings:

Jerry Bentley, *Humanists and Holy Writ: New Testament Scholarship in the Renaissance.*

Anthony Grafton and Lisa Jardine, *From Humanism to the Humanities: Education and the Liberal Arts in Fifteenth- and Sixteenth-Century Europe.*

Erika Rummel, *The Humanist-Scholastic Debate in the Renaissance and Reformation.*

Questions to Consider:

1. Were Humanists and the Italian Renaissance more modern than medieval or more medieval than modern?

2. If Thomas Aquinas had been alive in the 14th century, would he have defended Scholastic theology against Humanism, and if so, on what grounds would he have done so?

Lecture Nineteen
The Fall of the Byzantine Empire

Scope: The eastern half of the Roman Empire outlived the western half by nearly 1,000 years; not until 1453 did the Byzantine Empire (as later historians dubbed the eastern Roman Empire) fall, when Ottoman Turks captured Constantinople. The Ottomans had emerged in Asia Minor along the Byzantine-Turkish frontier in the early 14th century, and well before the fall of Constantinople in 1453, the Ottomans had expanded into southeastern Europe. Their defeats of crusader armies at the Battles of Nicopolis (1396) and Varna (1444) cemented their gains and guaranteed Islam a prominent place in subsequent Balkan and European history. Symbolically, though, the conquest of Constantinople and the Byzantine Empire marked the Ottomans' greatest victory. When Byzantine scholars emigrated to Italy afterward, this final collapse of the eastern half of the Roman Empire helped to fuel the antique revival then taking place in the west.

Outline

I. Although the Byzantine Empire and western Europe had once been part of a single Roman Empire, by the Late Middle Ages they had diverged in language and religion, and its geographical position made the Byzantine Empire both rich and vulnerable.

   A. Since the 6th century, the official language of the Byzantine Empire had been Greek, and since the middle of the 11th century, its official religion was Orthodox Christianity (as opposed to Catholic Christianity).

   B. Located at the point where Asia, Africa, and Europe meet, the Byzantine Empire profited from the trade that passed through it but also faced military threats from multiple directions.
   1. Turkish invasions of the 11th century had prompted the Byzantine Empire to call on western Europe for military assistance. The result was the First Crusade of 1095.
   2. The crusades failed to heal the divisions between Byzantium and the west—indeed, the Fourth Crusade in 1204 attacked

and captured Constantinople, which remained under crusader control until 1261.

II. The Ottoman Turks succeeded where everyone else had failed in the permanent acquisition of Constantinople and the Byzantine Empire. That success was the result of a long period of Ottoman growth and expansion.

    A. The Ottomans, whose name derives from an early ruler named Osman, emerged in Asia Minor along the Byzantine frontier.

    B. Under Osman, who died c. 1324, the Ottomans began to make permanent acquisitions and to abandon their nomadic origins, establishing the foundations for the later Ottoman state.

    C. A century before they captured Constantinople, the Ottomans had already captured territory in southeastern Europe, taking the fortress of Gallipoli in 1354 and the city of Adrianople in 1361.

    D. A few years after the capture of Adrianople, the Ottomans established their capital there, signaling that European expansion would be an important part of Ottoman policy.

    E. After the Ottomans defeated the Kingdom of Serbia at the First Battle of Kosovo (1389), Turkish Muslims began to emigrate to the Balkans in significant numbers.

    F. Ottoman success can be attributed to a number of factors, some of which distinguish them from their Turkish rivals.

        1. The Ottomans practiced unigeniture, bequeathing the whole of their empire to a single heir, which allowed the Ottomans to consolidate their gains effectively.

        2. The Ottomans' initial location on the periphery of the Islamic and Byzantine worlds allowed them to escape the notice of rivals until the Ottomans were ready to challenge them.

        3. The Ottomans mobilized Muslim support by making the concept of *gaza*, which involves fighting on behalf of Islam and for that religion's benefit, increasingly central to their self-image.

III. During the late 14th century and the first half of the 15th century, western Europeans organized crusades whose purpose was to halt the Ottomans' expansion and expel them from southeastern Europe, but the Ottomans beat back those crusades sent against them.

A. As early as the 1360s, Byzantine emperors traveled to the west, seeking the assistance of crusaders and offering to end the schism between Orthodox and Catholic Christianity.

B. The Hundred Years War and the Great Papal Schism made organizing a crusade to assist the Byzantines very difficult.

C. When a crusading army finally came and besieged the city of Nicopolis in 1396, it was badly defeated by the Ottomans.

IV. Following the Battle of Nicopolis, the Byzantine Empire enjoyed a precarious existence for two more generations, until the Ottoman Emperor Mehmed II finally captured Constantinople in 1453.

A. Early in the 15th century, the Ottomans faced an unexpected attack by central Asian nomads led by Tamerlane, briefly drawing the Ottomans' attention away from the Byzantines.

B. After the Ottomans captured the second largest Byzantine city, Thessalonica, in 1430, a Byzantine emperor again traveled to the west seeking aid and promising the union of the Orthodox and Catholic Churches. A crusading army was organized but defeated by the Ottomans at the Battle of Varna.

C. The Ottoman Emperor Mehmed II proclaimed the conquest of Constantinople to be central to the Ottomans' historical mission; by making effective use of artillery and moving more speedily than his predecessors had, he succeeded in capturing Constantinople in May 1453. The city became the new capital of the Ottoman Empire.

V. Although western Europe had rejoiced when Constantinople had fallen to the Fourth Crusade in 1204, it was dismayed by the news of the Ottoman conquest of Constantinople.

A. Culturally, Humanist scholars were concerned about the possible loss of works of ancient literature.

B. Politically, Europeans perceived that with the buffer of the Byzantine Empire removed, they were now more vulnerable to Ottoman invasion. The Ottoman landing at Otranto in southern Italy in 1480 seemed to confirm that vulnerability.

C. The cultural fears of the Humanists, however, were not realized.

1. Previous contacts between Byzantine and Humanist scholars had helped to transfer Greek knowledge to the west before the fall of Constantinople.
2. After the fall of the Byzantine Empire, Greek émigrés brought with them to Italy their knowledge of Classical antiquity.

Suggested Readings:

Franz Babinger, *Mehmed II and His Times.*

Nancy Bisaha, *Creating East and West: Renaissance Humanists and the Ottoman Turks.*

Cemal Kafadar, *Between Two Worlds: The Construction of the Ottoman State.*

Donald M. Nichol, *The End of the Byzantine Empire.*

Questions to Consider:

1. Was there any possibility of the Byzantine Empire surviving the Late Middle Ages, or was its demise largely a foregone conclusion?
2. If you asked a randomly chosen college student to identify the Byzantine Empire or the Ottoman Empire, would he or she be able to do so? Why would or wouldn't a student be able to make this identification?

Lecture Twenty
Ferdinand and Isabella

Scope: In 1469, Ferdinand, heir to the throne in the Kingdom of Aragon, married Isabella, heir to the throne in the Kingdom of Castile, setting the stage for one of the most important political events of the late 15th century: the dynastic unification of most of present-day Spain. Although the Kingdom of Aragon and the Kingdom of Castile remained separate entities even after Isabella and Ferdinand had inherited their respective thrones in 1474 and 1479, their marriage unified Christian Spain to an extent not seen since the 8th century. Ferdinand and Isabella promoted the unification of the Iberian Peninsula in other ways, such as by sponsoring the conquest of the last Islamic kingdom in Spain, the Kingdom of Granada, as well as by expelling the Jews from their kingdoms and the Muslims from Castile.

Outline

I. Since the Early Middle Ages, the Iberian Peninsula had been divided among Christian and Muslim rulers.

   A. During the course of the High Middle Ages, the Christian kingdoms of Spain (chiefly Castile, Aragon, Portugal, and Navarre) had expanded at the expense of Muslim Spain, so that by the middle of the 13th century, only the Kingdom of Granada in the far south remained under Muslim rulers.

   B. Spain's religious complexity matched its political complexity, as the Iberian Peninsula had sizable Christian, Jewish, and Muslim populations.

   C. Although Christian kingdoms could unite against their Muslim neighbors, they also fought among themselves, for example, during the War of the Two Peters, which ran from the 1350s into the 1380s.

II. The proximate cause for the marriage of Ferdinand and Isabella, and the dynastic union of Aragon and Castile, was the Catalonian Civil War of 1462 to 1472.

A. In 1462, a civil war broke out in the region of Catalonia, which was part of the Kingdom of Aragon. This civil war, fought largely over the issue of serfdom, pitted the king of Aragon and the peasantry against the kingdom's nobles and townspeople.

B. The king of Aragon, John II, sought Castilian assistance, and to that end, he arranged to have his heir, Ferdinand, marry Isabella, sister of the king of Castile, Henry IV.

    1. The marriage took place in 1469, and three years later, the civil war came to a temporary halt.

    2. Because Henry IV had no male sons and a single daughter who may have been illegitimate, there was a good chance that Isabella would eventually become queen of Castile.

C. In 1474, after Henry IV died, Isabella claimed the Castilian throne; after five years of fighting and with the support of her husband against Henry IV's daughter, she made good that claim.

D. Ferdinand became king of Aragon in 1479.

III. Because of the circumstances under which the marriage had been arranged, Isabella retained a great deal of autonomy, and Castile and Aragon remained distinct entities.

A. During the negotiations leading up to her marriage, Isabella and Castile more generally were in a strong position: The king of Aragon needed Castilian assistance and Isabella had other suitors.

B. Even after both Isabella and Ferdinand had become monarchs, Castile and Aragon retained their own parliamentary institutions, and even though Ferdinand was permitted to use the title "king of Castile," Isabella continued to sign royal decrees there.

C. Under the terms of Isabella's will, drawn up in 1504, Ferdinand had to surrender the title "king of Castile" after Isabella's death, and the title passed instead to their daughter.

IV. During their own lifetimes, Ferdinand and Isabella were hailed throughout Europe for having completed the Christian reconquest of the Iberian Peninsula.

A. Although the Kingdom of Granada was small compared to its Christian neighbors, its mountainous terrain, proximity to North African allies, and willingness to pay tribute to Christian rulers allowed it to survive into the late 15th century.

B. Because Castile and the Kingdom of Aragon had recently experienced divisive civil wars, Ferdinand and Isabella may have pursued the conquest of the Kingdom of Granada largely because of the prestige that it would confer upon them.

C. The conquest began in earnest in 1482. Granada's mountainous terrain favored the defenders and made the conquest difficult; not until 1492, after 10 trying years, did Ferdinand and Isabella finally succeed in taking the city of Granada and the Alhambra fortress.

D. In 1494, the pope bestowed the title "Catholic Monarchs" on Ferdinand and Isabella to reward them for completing the conquest of Granada. Europeans, keenly aware of Ottoman gains in southeastern Europe, welcomed the news of Christian victory in southwestern Europe.

V. Within a year of the conquest of Granada, Ferdinand and Isabella had expelled the Jews from those territories under their control, thus beginning the Sephardic Diaspora.

A. In March 1492, Ferdinand and Isabella ordered all Jews who refused to convert to Christianity to leave within four months.

B. The Muslims of Castile were expelled in 1502, and in 1525, the Muslims of the Kingdom of Aragon were likewise ordered to leave by the end of January 1526.

C. Whether Ferdinand and Isabella had long intended to expel the Jews once Granada had fallen, or whether they suddenly decided to do so in the euphoric aftermath of that event, is still an open question.

D. In ordering the expulsion of the Jews, Ferdinand and Isabella claimed that their presence was causing Jews who had converted to Christianity to lapse back into Judaism. Given the religious history of 15th-century Spain, Ferdinand and Isabella's concern about this phenomenon was probably genuine, though not necessarily well founded.

Suggested Readings:

John Edwards, *Ferdinand and Isabella*.

Henry Kamen, *Spain, 1469–1714: A Society of Conflict*, 3rd ed.

Peggy K. Liss, *Isabel the Queen: Life and Times*, rev. ed.

Questions to Consider:

1. In what ways has the modern history of Spain been shaped by the marriage of Ferdinand and Isabella and the circumstances of that marriage?

2. If Isabella had accepted the marriage proposals of her French suitor or her Portuguese suitor, how might the subsequent history of Spain and Europe have turned out differently?

Lecture Twenty-One
The Spanish Inquisition

Scope: In 1478, Ferdinand and Isabella sought and received papal permission to establish the Spanish Inquisition. Variously organized inquisitions had existed in Europe since the late 12th century, and the methods and procedures employed by the Spanish Inquisition differed little from those of its predecessors. In some respects, though, the Spanish Inquisition was different from what had come before. Ferdinand and Isabella, and all subsequent Spanish monarchs, maintained an unusual degree of royal control over the Spanish Inquisition, whose foundation was linked to a peculiarly Spanish situation: the large number of Spain's *conversos*, or Jews who had converted to Christianity, especially during and after the shockingly violent pogroms of 1391. Spanish inquisitors were especially interested in the religiosity of the *conversos* and most likely played some role in Ferdinand and Isabella's decision to expel the Jews in 1492.

Outline

I. During the 14th century, Jewish-Christian relations in Spain turned increasingly violent.

   A. The coming of bubonic plague in 1348 touched off pogroms in Spanish towns, and further attacks, often linked to accusations of host desecration, occurred in the 1360s and 1370s.

   B. The pogroms of 1391, however, greatly surpassed previous attacks in their intensity and were followed by decades of lower-level but still intimidating violence against Jews.

II. During and after the pogroms of 1391, Jews in large number converted to Christianity. The place of the *conversos* in Spanish society became a bitterly contested issue during the 15th century.

   A. Some *conversos* were able to achieve positions of considerable prominence, even becoming Christian bishops.

   B. Some Christians doubted the sincerity of the *conversos'* conversion, however, and accused them of "Judaizing," that is, secretly retaining Jewish beliefs and rituals while professing to be Christian.

C. After anti-*converso* rioting at Toledo in 1449, the town's governor issued an edict that forbade *conversos* to hold public or church offices and imposed the same restrictions on all who were descended from *conversos*.

D. Local and, eventually, royal laws imposed similar restrictions on *conversos* and their descendants.

    1. In doing so, these laws defined Jewishness not as a matter of a religious belief but as a matter of blood and biological descent.

    2. The notion of "purity of blood," defined as the absence of any Jewish ancestry, became a matter of importance in Spain for centuries to come.

III. Inquisitors were charged with identifying and correcting heretics. Because *conversos* were Christians who had undergone baptism, they came under the jurisdiction of inquisitors in a way that Jews (except for those who fostered heresy in Christians) did not.

A. Before 1478, inquisitions had played a minor role in Spanish history—they had never been employed in Castile and had played a circumscribed role elsewhere.

B. In 1478, Ferdinand and Isabella asked and received papal permission to establish inquisitors in the lands under their control.

    1. The right of Spanish monarchs to appoint inquisitors was unusual, and Ferdinand and Isabella foiled papal attempts to assert the papacy's control over the inquisition in Spain.

    2. In 1488, Ferdinand and Isabella established a governing council, the *Suprema*, to supervise inquisitors and to assist Spain's Inquisitor General. The members of the *Suprema* were chosen by the king or queen.

IV. Despite its lurid reputation for unparalleled cruelty, the Spanish Inquisition used standard inquisitorial techniques and procedures, which admittedly, left defendants at a grave disadvantage.

A. Inquisitors collected information by interrogating individuals and through the use of secret informers.

B. Inquisitors sequestered the goods of suspects and could hold suspects indefinitely before trial.

C. Hearings were carried out in secret, and the suspect was informed of specific charges only at the outset of the trial, which made organizing a defense difficult.

D. Suspects could clear themselves of suspicion if they could prove that those who had provided damning testimony hated them.

   1. However, inquisitors did not provide the names of witnesses to the suspect.

   2. Inquisitors could withhold any information and evidence from the defendants that might allow them to deduce the identities of witnesses.

E. In cases where oral testimony was deemed insufficient, inquisitors could have suspects tortured (though using techniques that were not unique to inquisitorial courts).

V. Inquisitorial trials could end in various ways.

   A. On rare occasions, inquisitors might proclaim the innocence of a defendant or allow him or her to go free after swearing an oath of innocence.

   B. Somewhat more commonly, inquisitors would rule that they lacked enough information to decide guilt or innocence and suspend the proceedings.

   C. In most cases, though, inquisitors found the defendant guilty.

   D. Punishments of the guilty were publicly announced and enacted at a ceremony known as an *auto-da-fé*.

      1. At an *auto-da-fé*, individuals who had confessed their guilt and had never previously been found guilty were assigned various penances to perform, such as wearing a distinctive garment called a *sanbenito*.

      2. Individuals who had been found guilty but continued to maintain their innocence, and individuals who had previously been convicted of heresy and had now been found guilty again, were handed over to secular authorities for execution on the spot.

VI. There is likely a connection between the emergence of the Spanish Inquisition in 1478 and the expulsion of the Jews in 1492.

   A. Since the earliest days of the Spanish Inquisition, some inquisitors had argued that it would be impossible to stamp out Jewish practices and beliefs among the *conversos* as long as Jews remained in Spain, encouraging Judaizing or at least serving as bad role models.

B. In the 1480s, regional expulsions of Jews had taken place in various parts of Spain, and some of these expulsions were carried out on the orders of local inquisitors.

Suggested Readings:

LuAnn Homza, ed., *The Spanish Inquisition: An Anthology of Sources, 1478–1614.*

Harvey Kamen, *The Spanish Inquisition: A Historical Revision.*

Teofilo Ruiz, *Spanish Society, 1400–1600.*

Questions to Consider:

1. Which aspect of inquisitorial procedure, if any, do you regard as the most unfair to the accused?

2. Historians have disagreed as to whether the *conversos* were truly "crypto-Jews" or whether the phenomenon of Judaizing was a figment of the inquisitorial and popular imagination. How can historians determine the correct answer to that question?

Lecture Twenty-Two
The Age of Exploration

Scope: During the course of the 15th century, Portuguese and Spanish explorers began to venture down the west coast of Africa and farther out into the Atlantic Ocean, reaching places where no European, to anyone's knowledge, had ever been before. This exploration was fueled by a desire to establish direct economic contact with sub-Saharan West Africa and with the Far East, thereby eliminating the need to rely on Arab middlemen; it was also fueled by the desire to establish contact with the imaginary Prester John, who was expected to help Christians in their wars against Muslims. Making use of a new type of boat, the *caravel*, by 1500, explorers had rounded the southern tip of Africa and reached the Americas. Both of these events would bring enormous economic benefits to Europe.

Outline

I.   Iberian sailors led the way in global exploration during the 15th century, and there are a number of reasons why Europeans in general, and Spanish and Portuguese especially, felt the need to undertake these voyages.

    A. Europeans wanted to establish direct economic contact with sub-Saharan West Africa and with the Far East to enable Europe to acquire the products of those regions without having to purchase them from Arab middlemen.

    B. The Iberian Peninsula, located only a dozen or so miles from North Africa, was ideally situated to take the lead in exploring the West African coast.

    C. Europeans, especially Iberians, believed (incorrectly) in the existence of a foreign ruler named Prester John, whom they expected to ally with Christians against Muslims once Europeans had located him and his kingdom.

    D. In the 15th century, Iberian sailors pioneered the use of a new type of vessel, the *caravel*, that made feasible long voyages down the coast of Africa or out into the Atlantic. The caravel used both square sails, which provided speed, and triangular lanteen sails, which provided maneuverability and allowed sailors to tack into the wind efficiently.

    E. Spanish sailors also had access to the best European mapmakers, who were to be found on the Balearic Islands in the Mediterranean.

II. During the course of the 15th century, Portuguese explorers, largely thanks to the encouragement of Prince Henry the Navigator, edged their way down the coast of West Africa, until in 1498, Vasco da Gama finally rounded the southern tip of Africa, the Cape of Good Hope.

    A. In 1415, a Portuguese army captured the town of Ceuta in Morocco. The conquest did not bring the expected financial rewards, however, because trade between Ceuta and sub-Saharan Africa was still in the hands of Arab merchants.

    B. Prince Henry the Navigator, son of the king of Portugal, took the lead in promoting the exploration of the West African coast.

        1. Prince Henry took part in the conquest of Ceuta, was head of a Portuguese military order called the Order of Christ, and was keenly interested in crusading activity.

        2. After the conquest of Ceuta, however, Portugal failed to gain any more ground in Morocco, and Henry became increasingly interested in studying navigation.

    C. Portuguese explorers, year after year, traveled a bit farther down the coast, establishing trading posts as they went.

        1. Portuguese explorers first went around Cape Bojador in 1434 but reached the mouth of the Congo River only in 1483.

        2. Bartholomew Diaz reached the southern tip of Africa in 1488, and a decade later, Vasco da Gama went around it.

        3. The Portuguese established their most important trading fort, Elmina, in 1482, whose primary purpose was to fend off Spanish rivals.

    D. The Portuguese, hoping to monopolize trade with sub-Saharan West Africa, tried to keep knowledge of their activities a secret, but Spanish explorers and merchants caught wind of what was happening and became rivals of the Portuguese.

E. Within two decades of Vasco da Gama's voyage around the Cape of Good Hope, the Portuguese were well on their way to establishing a monopoly over trade in the Indian Ocean.

   1. The Portuguese destroyed the ships of rival Arab traders whenever possible and required those whom they spared to purchase licenses from the Portuguese permitting them to trade.

   2. The Portuguese seized key bases for themselves, such as Goa (off the coast of India) in 1510, Malacca (in Malaysia) in 1511, and Hormuz (at the mouth of the Persian Gulf) in 1515.

   3. The Portuguese established a small trading post at Macau in China in 1557.

III. Even as some Portuguese sailors were making their way down the coast of West Africa, other Portuguese and Spanish sailors were venturing out into the Atlantic Ocean, colonizing islands through methods that would soon be used on a much vaster scale in the Americas.

   A. In the early 14th century, Genoese sailors unexpectedly stumbled on the Canary Islands, much to the amazement of contemporary Europeans.

   1. Between 1402 and 1496, the Castilians conquered the Canary Islands. The native population, the Guanches, was decimated by disease, and Castilians imported West African slaves to provide labor on the sugar plantations they established on the Canaries.

   2. Because a substantial number of Spanish settlers came to the Canary Islands, West African slave labor did not become as important there as it would later be in the Americas.

   3. The Canary Islands were a useful base for explorers wishing to voyage even farther out into the Atlantic.

   B. The Portuguese colonized the previously uninhabited Madeira Islands in the 15th century—establishing sugar plantations, vineyards, and wineries there—as well as the Azores, which the Portuguese used to grow food for the inhabitants of the Canary and Madeira Islands.

Suggested Readings:

Felipe Fernández-Armesto, *Before Columbus: Exploration and Colonization from the Mediterranean to the Atlantic, 1229–1492.*

Peter Russell, *Prince Henry the Navigator.*

A. J. R. Russell-Wood, *The Portuguese Empire, 1415–1808: A World on the Move.*

Questions to Consider:

1. How does knowledge of the prior Portuguese/Spanish colonization of the Atlantic Islands change our understanding of the subsequent colonization of the Americas?

2. Given the economic consequences of European colonization in the Americas and European domination of trade in the Indian Ocean, should the 1490s be regarded as *the* moment when Europe began to outstrip its rivals decisively in wealth and power?

Lecture Twenty-Three
Columbus and the Columbian Exchange

Scope: Christopher Columbus's voyage to the Americas in 1492, undertaken with the support of Ferdinand and Isabella, marks a turning point not just in European history but in global history. Although Columbus, to the day he died, denied that the continents he had encountered were anything other than Asia, other Europeans quickly deduced that they were a *mundus novus*, a "new world," whose existence had previously been unknown. Although Columbus's personal fortunes waned beginning with his second voyage to the Americas in 1493, during the course of the 16th century, Spain conquered both the Aztec Empire in Mesoamerica and the Inca Empire of South America, which in turn, facilitated the extraction of the mineral and agricultural wealth of the Americas. More broadly, contact between the Americas and Europe initiated a process called the *Columbian Exchange*: a massive trading of plants, animals, and diseases between the Americas and Europe that left both forever changed.

Outline

I.   Columbus was not the first sailor to try to venture across the Atlantic Ocean. What set Columbus apart from others was his determination not to turn back until he had succeeded.

   A. Columbus came from Genoa in Italy and moved to Portugal around 1476, where he learned how to captain his own ship, sailing around the Atlantic to West Africa and, perhaps, to Iceland, among other places.

   B. Columbus underestimated the size of the Atlantic Ocean. He also mistakenly believed that Japan was some 1,500 miles off the coast of China and, therefore, a destination that could be easily reached for provisioning his ships.

   C. After the king of Portugal refused to support Columbus, he traveled to Castile in 1485, where he spent the next seven years lobbying Ferdinand and Isabella.

1. Ferdinand and Isabella were occupied with the conquest of the Kingdom of Granada, but three months after its fall in January 1492, they finally gave Columbus three ships and crews.
2. Columbus and his ships left the Canary Islands in September 1492, and after a 33-day voyage, they reached the Bahamas.

II. Although the Bahamas did not match his expectations, when Columbus returned to Europe, he still gave glowing reports about what he had found.

   A. Columbus failed to find in the Caribbean the cities, gold, and spices for which he was looking.

   B. When he returned to Europe in 1493, he nevertheless told Ferdinand and Isabella, in a letter circulated throughout Europe, that he had found large amounts of gold and spices.

   C. Technically, by virtue of a treaty between Portugal and Spain and an earlier papal proclamation, the lands discovered by Columbus should have gone to Portugal.
   1. The pope at that moment, however, came from Aragon, and he failed to back the Portuguese claim.
   2. As a result, Portugal and Spain agreed to the Treaty of Tordesillas in 1494, which drew a line about 1,450 miles to the west of the Azores, granting Portugal control over any part of the New World to the right of that line and Spain control over any part to the left.

   D. In 1504, the author Amerigo Vespucci published a book called *Mundus novus*, which popularized the view that Columbus had found lands not previously known to Europeans.

III. Columbus's return to Europe in 1493 marks the highpoint of his career; his three subsequent voyages across the Atlantic (in 1493, 1498, and 1502) did not turn out so well.

   A. In 1493, Columbus brought a large fleet to the island of Hispaniola, where he had left some of his crew after their ship had foundered during the first voyage.
   1. The crew he had left behind was missing and presumably dead.
   2. On this voyage, Columbus and his fellow travelers encountered the cannibal Caribs. The cannibalism of some

Caribbean groups made an unfavorable impression on the Europeans, as did their near nakedness.

    3. Some of the settlers on the second voyage seized their ships and returned to Spain, where their description of the New World differed considerably from Columbus's.

B. Columbus had a much harder time finding recruits willing to accompany him on his third voyage in 1498, during which a royal official arrested him for maladministration and sent him back to Europe, where Ferdinand and Isabella forbade him ever to go to Hispaniola again.

C. By the time of his fourth voyage in 1502, Columbus was able to secure only poor ships and crews, although he did reach the coast of Central America during this voyage.

D. Columbus died in 1506, still trying to win back the position of favor he had lost.

E. Further explorations demonstrated that Columbus was wrong when he claimed to have reached Asia.

    1. In 1513, Núñez de Balboa crossed the Isthmus of Panama and spied the Pacific Ocean.

    2. Between 1519 and 1522, ships commanded by Ferdinand Magellan circumnavigated the globe.

F. In Mesoamerica and South America, the Spanish encountered the Aztec Empire, which Hernándo Cortes conquered between 1519 and 1521, and the Inca Empire, conquered under the leadership of Francisco Pizarro between 1531 and the late 1560s.

IV. The speed and relative ease with which the Spanish conquered both the Aztecs and the Incas was a consequence of the devastating impact that European diseases had on the natives of the Americas. This exchange of diseases was part of a broader biological event known as the *Columbian Exchange.*

A. Because they had been almost completely isolated from Asia, Africa, and Europe for some 10,000 to 12,000 years, the natives of the Americas lacked immunity against those diseases that had accumulated in the European disease pool during that time.

    1. Smallpox was the disease that wreaked the most havoc among the natives of the Americas, but it was only one of many such illnesses.

2. The Americas, too, had diseases unfamiliar to Europeans, most notably syphilis, but that disease had relatively limited demographic consequences.

3. Within a few generations of Columbus's voyage, the populations of Mesoamerica and South America had probably fallen by 70 to 90 percent.

B. With regard to plants and crops, both the Americas and Europe were greatly changed by the Columbian Exchange.

1. In the Americas, Europeans encountered potatoes and maize, which would eventually become, along with the traditional wheat, basic staples for Europeans.

2. Europeans brought sugar cane, bananas, and coffee beans to the Americas.

C. With regard to animals, the Columbian Exchange had a much greater impact on the Americas than it did on Europe. Europeans introduced horses, sheep, pigs, and cattle to the Americas; these animals soon altered the ecology of the Americas drastically.

D. Although the Spanish failed to find the gold and spices that Columbus had initially sought, South American silver and agricultural products quickly became significant sources of wealth.

Suggested Readings:

Noble David Cook, *Born to Die: Disease and the New World Conquest, 1492–1650.*

Alfred W. Crosby, *The Columbian Exchange: Biological and Cultural Consequences of 1492 (30th Anniversary Edition).*

Anthony Grafton, April Shelford, and Nancy Siraisi, *New Worlds, Ancient Texts: The Power of Tradition and the Shock of Discovery.*

William D. Phillips, Jr., and Carla Rahn Phillips, *The Worlds of Christopher Columbus.*

Questions to Consider:

1. Which events during the last 500 years, if any, have equaled Columbus's voyage to the Americas with regard to their material and intellectual consequences?

2. Columbus is the only late-medieval individual to have a national holiday named after him in the United States and elsewhere in the Americas (except Venezuela, which has replaced Columbus Day with Indigenous Resistance Day). Should Columbus Day be celebrated as a national holiday in the United States, as it has been since 1937? Is there someone else from the Late Middle Ages or the Middle Ages more generally to whom you would dedicate a national holiday if you could?

Lecture Twenty-Four
When Did the Middle Ages End?

Scope: Although the Humanists of the Italian Renaissance came to believe
that they had brought the Middle Ages to an end, there are reasons
to dispute that claim. In terms of politics, economics,
demographics, social organization, and everyday life, Humanism
and the Italian Renaissance occasioned no fundamental break with
the past; even with regard to culture, there was substantial
continuity. It might be better to conceive of the Middle Ages as
having ended during a long period that lasted for many centuries—
and to identify the crucial turning point in this process, which is
still ongoing, as having occurred during the second half of the 18th
century and the first half of the 19th century.

Outline

I. Identifying those characteristics that defined the Middle Ages as
    "medieval" is a subjective undertaking, but it must be done if one is to
    attempt to answer the question: When did the Middle Ages end?

    A. Regarding government, monarchy (usually in its hereditary form)
    was the dominant form in the Middle Ages.

    B. Regarding the economy, it was fundamentally agrarian—farming
    was the occupation of the great majority of workers.
    Manufacturing was small-scale, carried out in home workshops by
    small groups who were, as often as not, related by blood and
    whose activities were regulated by guilds. Merchants tried to
    maximize their profit margins rather than the number of sales.

    C. Regarding society, the elite consisted of a hereditary warrior
    nobility that enjoyed specific legal privileges; this nobility
    maintained its position of superiority through its stone castles and
    knightly fighting techniques. At the bottom were serfs, owned and
    unfree peasants who were subjected to various legal disabilities
    and whose status was hereditary.

    D. Regarding culture and thought, Catholic Christianity was the
    dominant religion, and intellectual life centered on the knowledge
    of God: Theological and biblical study were regarded as the

highest forms of intellectual pursuit. Reverence for the intellectual authorities of the ancient world, such as Aristotle, was so great that the acquisition of knowledge in every field was equated with mastering ancient texts.

E. Regarding demography, fertility rates and mortality rates, especially infant mortality rates, were high. Typically, one-quarter of all children died within the first year of life and another quarter before puberty. Average life expectancy was somewhere between 30 and 35; living much past 60 was not common.

F. Note that these characteristics did not come into existence all at once. The demographic and economic characteristics were as true of antiquity as of the Middle Ages, and ancient Rome had been monarchical since the time of Augustus. Not until the High Middle Ages were these characteristics all in place.

II. The characteristics listed above still applied to Europe in 1500, the traditional date given for the end of the Late Middle Ages. However, late-medieval developments set the stage for subsequent changes that would mark a more definitive break with the past.

A. Humanism, in arguing that human beings could and should achieve earthly happiness, laid the groundwork for scrutiny of all institutions to determine whether they, in fact, contributed to human happiness and for rejection of any institutions failing to pass that test. In doing so, Humanism made it possible to conceive of change as essentially good rather than bad.

B. The Columbian Exchange, which gave Europeans access to new staple crops (maize and the potato), laid the groundwork for a modern demographic system characterized by low mortality and low fertility rates.

C. By revealing the deficiencies of ancient texts, both the dissections carried out in the name of Renaissance art and Columbus's encounter with the Americas called into question the idea that old texts were the best sources of knowledge.

III. Although the 16th and 17th centuries are conventionally considered to lie beyond the Middle Ages, one can argue that, in fact, they remained essentially medieval, even as the process of disengagement with the Middle Ages continued and gained momentum.

A. The Scientific Revolution of the 16th and 17th centuries, exemplified by the works of such individuals as Copernicus and Newton, further called into question the accuracy of ancient texts and lent strong support to the notion that empirical observation was the surest basis of human knowledge. That realization, in turn, caused the natural sciences to overtake theology as the most respected academic field.

B. The discovery that the universe operates according to mathematical laws made God seem more remote than had been the case before; direct divine intervention came to be understood as exceptional rather than frequent or constant.

C. The Protestant Reformation of the 16th century ended the near universality of Catholicism in Europe.

D. Nonetheless, despite these breaks with the past, the period of the Middle Ages was not over in the 1500s and 1600s.

  1. The Protestant Reformation should be understood as fundamentally medieval in nature: The central questions at stake were theological and biblical.

  2. Every scientist associated with the Scientific Revolution was a Christian who accepted the existence of God and the reality of miracles.

  3. Politically, economically, socially, and demographically, the 1500s and 1600s still reveal the characteristics associated with the Middle Ages.

IV. Between 1750 and 1850, intellectual and cultural changes combined with changes in every facet of human existence to create a world that, at long last, was more unlike than like the Middle Ages.

  A. Intellectually, the 18th-century Enlightenment shifted the debate from such questions as "Which variant of Christianity is the best?" and "What is God's will for humanity?" to "Do miracles and God exist, and are revealed religions, including Christianity, Judaism, and Islam, sources of good or harm to society?"

  B. The French Revolution of 1789–1799 established the First Republic in France; thereafter, the central issue in European political life was the rise of democracy and mass political participation.

C. The French Revolution abolished serfdom, guilds, and noble privileges, initiating a process whereby all three subsequently vanished throughout Europe.

D. The emergence of liberalism as a self-conscious ideology in the first half of the 19th century, with its advocacy of broader political participation, free economic markets, and maximal individual liberty, continued this trend away from the Middle Ages.

E. Demographically, starting in the first half of the 18th century, mortality rates began to drop in the wealthier parts of Europe, with fertility rates to follow a few generations afterward.

   1. The agricultural revolution of the 18th century increased the European food supply and made it much more reliable.

   2. Edward Jenner's experiments with smallpox inoculation allowed humans to begin to protect themselves against disease in ways never before possible.

F. The period from 1750 to 1850 also saw changes in where people lived, how they lived, and how they worked.

   1. Industrialization resulted in massive urbanization; by 1851, England had more urban dwellers than rural dwellers, and other industrializing countries likewise experienced the explosive growth of cities and a dwindling peasantry.

   2. The movement of people, goods, and information over land had barely changed since antiquity, but the invention of the steamboat, the railroad, and the telegraph in the first half of the 19th century began the process whereby human beings experienced the constraints of time and space in ways unimaginable to those who had lived before.

Suggested Readings:

Marcus Bull, *Thinking Medieval: An Introduction to the Study of the Middle Ages*.

John van Engen, ed., *The Past and Future of Medieval Studies*.

Questions to Consider:

1. What objections could and should be raised against the argument that the Middle Ages did not really end until the period 1750–1850?

2. In the May/June 2006 issue of *Foreign Affairs*, journalist and political scientist John Rapley published an essay called "The New Middle Ages," which argues that:

> The Middle Ages ended when the rise of capitalism on a national scale led to powerful states with sovereignty over particular territories and populations. Now that capitalism is operating globally, those states are eroding and a new medievalism is emerging, marked by multiple and overlapping sovereignties and identities—particularly in the developing world, where states were never strong in the first place.

To what extent do you agree or disagree with this analysis?

Timeline

1337	Outbreak of the Hundred Years War.
1340	King Edward III of England revives his claim to the French throne and uses the title "king of France" for himself.
1346	The English defeat the French at the Battle of Crécy.
1347–1351	First outbreak of the Black Death.
1349	Death of William Ockham.
1351	Statute of Labourers enacted in England; orders that wages be frozen at pre-plague levels.
1356	The English defeat the French at the Battle of Poitiers and take the king of France captive.
1357	The Parisian merchant Etienne Marcel and his followers seize control of Paris.
1358	Outbreak of the French peasant revolt known as the *Jacquerie*; it and the revolt of Etienne Marcel are suppressed.
1360	England and France agree to the Treaty of Brétigny, which brings the Hundred Years War to a temporary halt.
1361	Black Death returns to Europe; for the next century or so, similar flare-ups of the Black Death will occur about once or twice a decade, on average.
1361	Ottomans capture Adrianople in southeastern Europe; it will become the new capital of their empire.
1369	Hundred Years War resumes.
1374	Death of Petrarch.

1377 .... Papacy returns to Rome from Avignon.

1377 .... Papal condemnation of articles drawn from the writings of John Wycliffe.

1378 .... Elections of Popes Urban VI and Clement VII; start of the Great Papal Schism.

1378–1382 .... Revolt of the *Ciompi* in Florence.

1380 .... Death of Catherine of Siena.

1381 .... English Peasants Revolt.

1384 .... Death of John Wycliffe.

1389 .... Ottomans defeat the Kingdom of Serbia at the First Battle of Kosovo.

1396 .... Ottomans defeat a crusading army at Nicopolis.

1396 .... France and England agree to the second major truce in the Hundred Years War.

1402 .... Castilians begin the conquest of the Canary Islands.

1409 .... Council of Pisa attempts but fails to end the Great Papal Schism by electing a third pope.

1413–1414 .... Oldcastle's Revolt (uprising of English Lollards).

1414–1417 .... Council of Constance meets and succeeds in ending the Great Papal Schism.

1415 .... Jan Hus condemned by the Council of Constance and burned to death for heresy.

1415 .... Hundred Years War resumes; English invade Normandy and defeat the French at the Battle of Agincourt.

1415	Portuguese conquer Ceuta in North Africa.
1419–1436	Hussite revolt in Bohemia.
1420	King Charles VI of France agrees to the Treaty of Troyes, which states that the next king of France should be the son of King Henry V of England.
1422	King Charles VI dies; France refuses to honor the Treaty of Troyes.
1429	Joan of Arc meets with the French heir to the throne, then rallies French forces at the siege of Orléans.
1429	The son of Charles VI of France has himself crowned as King Charles VII of France, in defiance of the Treaty of Troyes.
1430	Death of Christine de Pizan.
1431	Joan of Arc captured by Burgundians and ransomed to the English, who execute her for witchcraft.
1431–1449	Council of Basel meets but experiences a schism when some of its members establish a rival council, first at Ferrara, then at Florence.
1434	Portuguese explorers round Cape Bojador in West Africa.
1440	Lorenzo Valla publishes his work demonstrating that the Donation of Constantine is not what it purports to be.
1440	Ottomans defeat crusaders at the Battle of Varna.

c. 1450 .... Kingdom of France establishes a standing royal army.

c. 1450 .... Johannes Gutenberg invents the printing press.

1453 .... Ottoman Emperor Mehmed II captures Constantinople and makes it the new capital of the Ottoman Empire.

1453 .... The effective end of the Hundred Years War.

1460 .... The papal bull *Execrabilis* reasserts the superiority of papal to conciliar authority by decreeing that papal rulings cannot be appealed to a council.

1462–1472 .... Civil war in Catalonia.

1469 .... Ferdinand, heir to the throne in the Kingdom of Aragon, marries Isabella, likely heir to the throne in the Kingdom of Castile.

1474 .... Isabella becomes queen of Castile but must spend the first five years of her reign fighting to make good on her claim.

1478 .... Establishment of the Spanish Inquisition.

1479 .... Ferdinand becomes king of Aragon.

1482 .... Ferdinand and Isabella begin the conquest of the Kingdom of Granada, the last Islamic kingdom on the Iberian Peninsula.

1482 .... Portuguese establish trading fort at Elmina on the coast of West Africa (present-day Ghana).

1484–1486	Civil war in Catalonia resumes and finally ends with the freeing of Catalonia's serfs.
1492	Fall of the Kingdom of Granada.
1492	Ferdinand and Isabella expel from their kingdoms all Jews who refuse to convert to Christianity.
1492	Columbus's first voyage to the Americas.
1497	Two inquisitors publish *Malleus maleficarum* (*Hammer of the Witches*), the most influential late-medieval treatise on witchcraft.
1498	Vasco da Gama rounds the southern tip of Africa and enters the Indian Ocean.
1502	Expulsion of the Muslims of Castile.
1516	Erasmus publishes his first version of the Latin Bible, revised on the basis of Greek manuscripts.
1519–1521	Spanish conquest of the Aztec Empire in Mesoamerica.
1519–1522	Ferdinand Magellan circumnavigates the globe.
1528	Baldassare Castiglione publishes *The Book of the Courtier*.
1531	Spanish conquest of the Inca Empire in South America begins.

Glossary

Babylonian Captivity: Term used by the Italian Humanist Petrarch to characterize the papal residence at Avignon during most of the 14th century. This characterization implied that popes were being held captive just as the Hebrews had been held captive in Babylon during the 6th century B.C. It reflected a general feeling that French influence over the church had grown too strong and that Rome was the natural and proper residence of popes, whose claims to primacy rested on their status as the direct successors of Saint Peter, believed to have been the first bishop of Rome.

Black Death: A term coined in the 16th and 17th centuries to describe the outbreak of disease that struck Europe between 1347 and 1351. Although the identification of the Black Death as plague, chiefly bubonic plague, is periodically challenged, at present, bubonic plague and other strains of plague remain the most likely candidates. The standard estimate is that one-third of Europe's population died between 1347 and 1351, but local research has consistently turned up higher mortality figures than that, and some historians now think it more likely that Europe lost one-half of its population. The Black Death returned to Europe in 1361 and kept coming back for centuries—the last major episode in western Europe dates to 1720, and it persisted in eastern Europe for more than a century beyond that.

caravel: A type of sailing vessel, devised by Iberian sailors in the 15th century, that made possible both regular long-distance ocean voyages and voyages down and up the west coast of Africa. By combining the use of square sails, which permit fast travel, and triangular lanteen sails, which make it easier to tack into the wind, caravels possessed the speed and maneuverability necessary to sail around the globe.

Ciompi: Unskilled wage laborers in the Florentine cloth industry. Together with other clothworkers, the *Ciompi* seized control of the government of Florence in 1378 and maintained control until 1382—a rare example of a successful urban revolt in which workers overthrew, even if only temporarily, the merchant plutocracies and oligarchies that routinely governed late-medieval towns.

Columbian Exchange: Refers to the transfer of plants, animals, and diseases between the Old World and the New World following Columbus's first voyage to the Americas in 1492. For all intents and purposes, the Old World and the New World had been out of contact with each other since the end of the last ice age, around 10,000 B.C.; in the meantime, the Old World and the New had developed different species of plants and animals, as well as diseases unique to their human populations. Europe, thanks to its contact with Asia and Africa, possessed a larger variety of diseases and domesticated animals than did the Americas, and once introduced to the Americas, those diseases and animals ran amok, bringing disaster to the inhabitants of the Americas. The acquisition of New World crops and the cultivation of Old World crops in the Americas brought enormous demographic and economic benefits to Europe.

conciliarism: Refers to the belief, which gained currency during the 14th and 15th centuries, that the supreme spiritual authority within the Catholic Church should reside not with the papacy but with general councils. With the decline of papal authority that accompanied the Babylonian Captivity and the Great Papal Schism, conciliarists proposed conciliarism as a solution to the era's problems. Although early-15th-century councils, such as the Council of Pisa and the Council of Constance, did wield considerable power, conciliarism failed to consolidate its gains, and the papal bull *Execrabilis*, issued in 1460, reiterated the authority of popes as superior to that of councils.

Dance of Death: A literary and artistic motif that shows the figure of Death, usually in the form of a skeleton, unexpectedly accosting people of all ages, sexes, and occupations, then leading them away. The appearance of this motif in the second half of the 14th century has been interpreted as reflecting a keener post-Black Death awareness of the possibility and the indiscriminateness of death and, perhaps, even indicating a macabre fascination with the subject.

flagellants: The use of self-flagellation as a penitential technique had been known during the High Middle Ages, when on rare occasions, bands of roving flagellants created public disturbances. As the Black Death struck Europe, flagellant bands assumed a new importance, one they would maintain for several generations. Flagellants hoped that by whipping themselves they could assuage God's anger, which they saw as responsible for bringing the Black Death to Europe. Contemporaries accused flagellants of attacking Catholic clerics and Jews, as they likely did, and authorities tried to stamp out these bands whenever possible.

Great (Papal) Schism: Not to be confused with the Great Schism of 1054, when Christianity split into its Orthodox and Catholic sects, the Great Papal

Schism refers to the period between 1378 and 1417 when rival lines of popes existed at Rome and at Avignon (and, as of 1409, a third line of popes existed at Pisa). European countries, towns, villages, and religious orders split over which of these papal lines was legitimate. The Council of Constance, which met from 1414 to 1417, finally brought the Great Papal Schism to a close, but by then, nearly 40 years had elapsed, during which time there had been no obvious head of the Catholic Church.

Humanism: In the context of late-medieval history and the Italian Renaissance, Humanism refers to an artistic and literary movement that called for a return to Classical norms and values—and, by extension, for a rejection of medieval art and literature. Humanists called upon artists to embrace naturalism in art and eschew the abstraction that they believed to be characteristic of medieval art; they called upon authors and readers to devote themselves to the study of Classical literature, to learn Greek, and to write Latin as it had been written in the days of Cicero. Humanists believed that the beauty of Classical literature was inspirational and a source of morality—it would move people to behave better, unlike Scholastic philosophy, which was too befuddling to be of any practical use.

Jacquerie: The peasant rebellion that took place in the regions around Paris in 1358. The opening decades of the Hundred Years War had resulted in substantial destruction in northern France, and when English forces captured the king of France at the Battle of Poitiers in 1356, the Kingdom of France was in turmoil. An attempt to force French peasants to rebuild destroyed castles touched off a spontaneous eruption of violence as French peasants attacked nobles in May and June 1358. The peasants also allied with the Parisian merchant Etienne Marcel and his followers, who had already seized control of Paris in a separate revolt. By the end of that summer, the French nobility had rallied and put down the *Jacquerie*, together with Etienne Marcel. The term *Jacquerie* comes from "Jacques Bonhomme," a generic name used of French peasants in the same way that "Joe Sixpack" is used of working-class Americans.

Lollards: A term of uncertain etymology, but perhaps meaning "mumbler," it is the name of those heretics in late-14th- and early-15th-century England who professed themselves to be followers of the Oxford theologian John Wycliffe. The most distinctive characteristic of the Lollards was their Bible reading; small groups of local Lollards would meet secretly to read and discuss the Bible, which might explain why they were regarded as "mumblers." Although initially the Lollards were a strongly pacifist group, in the wake of prosecutions, some Lollards embraced violent resistance, which resulted in Lollard uprisings, such as Oldcastle's Revolt in 1413–1414. Although the Lollard revolts were, compared to other heretical uprisings, poorly organized and easily dealt with, they nonetheless increased suspicion of Lollardy.

Ottomans: Refers to the Turkish dynasty established by Osman, who died c. 1324, and to those Turks who accepted that dynasty as their rulers. The Ottoman dynasty emerged along the Turkish-Byzantine frontier in western Asia Minor and soon became the chief Muslim foe of the Byzantine Empire and of western crusading armies sent to halt the Ottoman advance. By 1361, the Ottomans had established a foothold in southeastern Europe and moved their capital there; when the Ottomans captured Constantinople in 1453, thereby bringing the Byzantine Empire to an end, they made that city their new capital.

Spanish Inquisition: Refers to the inquisition established in 1478 by Ferdinand and Isabella in the kingdoms under their control. The purpose of the Spanish Inquisition, like all the inquisitions that had existed since the late 12th century in various parts of Europe, was to identify heretics and get them to recognize their error. Those who were convicted of heresy but refused to recant were handed over to secular authorities for execution, as were relapsed heretics. The investigative techniques used by the Spanish Inquisition were not different from the techniques used by other inquisitorial courts; by the 15th century, secular law courts, too, had adopted many of those same techniques. What made the Spanish Inquisition distinctive was the degree of royal control that Ferdinand and Isabella, and Spanish rulers after them, exercised over the institution, as well as the Inquisition's strong and specific interest in "Judaizing," that is, in Christians who had converted from Judaism and the descendants of such Christians (*conversos*), who were suspected of secretly clinging to Jewish beliefs and rituals.

Templars: A military order established in the early 12th century. The initial mission of the Templars was to protect pilgrims in the Holy Land, but they came to be identified generally with the defense of the crusader states and of Jerusalem. As members of a military order, Templars were warriors who followed a monastic lifestyle. By 1300, the Templars had grown wealthy but were intensely criticized for their failures to keep Jerusalem and the crusader states in Christian hands. In 1307, King Philip IV of France ordered the arrest of all the Templars in France and the seizure of their property, urged other European monarchs to do likewise, and leveled extraordinary accusations of sodomy and blasphemy against the Templars. Although the Templars were theoretically answerable only to the pope, Philip IV went ahead with his trial of the French Templars, and in 1312, Pope Clement V ordered that all Templar houses in Europe be disbanded.

transi tomb: A type of funereal monument that emerged in the 14th century and achieved a certain level of popularity in subsequent centuries. The transi tomb depicts the deceased not in peaceful repose, as had previously been the norm, but as a grotesque corpse in an advanced state of decay. Some transi tombs bear two likenesses of the deceased: one on the top, where the dead person lies in peaceful repose; and one on the bottom, where he or she lies as a rotting corpse, sometimes in the process of being consumed by vermin. Some cultural historians have seen the emergence of transi tombs as evidence of a macabre late-medieval sensibility that emerged in a world where the Black Death made death an inescapable presence.

witch: As defined in the Late Middle Ages, a combination of a heretic and a maleficent magician. Witches derive their magical powers from Satan, whom they worship and with whom they enter into an explicit compact. Belief in the existence of magicians who used their powers to harm others long predates the Middle Ages, and a belief that heretics formed an orgiastic, devil-worshipping sub-society existed throughout the Middle Ages; it was only during the Late Middle Ages that the concept of the heretic and of the maleficent magician fused and became the "witch." The study of inquisitorial court records suggests that this fusion first took place in those courts themselves, then spread outward into society. Although the number of witch trials in late-medieval Europe was small compared to the number of such trials in 16th- and 17th-century Europe, by 1500, the witch had become a well-defined idea whose existence was accepted seemingly by most (though certainly not all), at all levels of society.

Biographical Notes

Boniface VIII: Pope from 1294 to 1303. Elected under unusual circumstances—his predecessor, Celestine V, was the only pope to have resigned voluntarily from office. Boniface VIII became embroiled in a fierce struggle with King Philip IV of France over, at first, the issue of royal taxation of the French clergy, then over the broader issue of the superiority of secular or ecclesiastical authority. Boniface VIII's papal bull of 1302, *Unam sanctam*, stated succinctly and clearly that popes had the right to judge and depose kings, not vice versa. After the seizure of Boniface VIII by his opponents at Anagni in 1303 and his death shortly after his release, the papacy backed away from the strong claims that Boniface VIII had made on behalf of the institution.

Catherine of Siena: An Italian mystic who lived from c. 1347 to 1380. Catherine of Siena played an active role in both the literary and the religious life of 14th-century Europe. Her hundreds of letters, written in Italian, hold an important place in the history of late-medieval vernacular literature, while her spectacular fasting and asceticism made her one of the most revered figures of the period, sometimes called upon to intervene in the day's most pressing political and religious conflicts. Catherine of Siena was canonized in 1461 and proclaimed a Doctor of the Church (one of the first two women to receive that title) in 1970.

Christine de Pizan: An author who lived from c. 1365 to 1430. Italian by birth but an inhabitant of France during her adult life, Christine de Pizan was quite possibly the first woman who supported herself and her family through her literary career. She wrote works of many different kinds, from poems to military treatises, but is best known today for her *Book of the City of Ladies* and her *Treasure of the City of Ladies*, which offer defenses of women against the charges that they are intellectually and morally inferior to men.

Christopher Columbus: An explorer; born in Genoa, Italy, in 1451, and died in Valladolid, Spain, in 1506. In 1485, having been rebuffed by the king of Portugal, Columbus approached the king and queen of Spain, asking for ships and crews that he would lead westward across the Atlantic Ocean and, so he hoped, to Asia, thereby creating a new trade route linking Europe to the Far East. In 1492, Columbus finally received the ships and crews, and he made the first of his four transatlantic voyages to the Americas—although he always publicly maintained that he had, in fact, reached Asia. Columbus's voyage to the Americas began the Columbian Exchange, that is, a massive transfer of plants, animals, and diseases between the Old World and the New World. It also called into question the knowledge of ancient geographers, who had not known about the existence of the continents that Columbus encountered.

Ferdinand and Isabella: Ferdinand was king of Aragon from 1479 to 1516; Isabella was queen of Castile from 1474 to 1504. Their marriage in 1469 paved the way for the dynastic union of the Kingdoms of Aragon and Castile, which nonetheless remained distinct, and brought about a greater degree of unity in Christian Spain. These monarchs were responsible for establishing the Spanish Inquisition in 1478; for overseeing the conquest of the last Muslim kingdom on the Iberian Peninsula, the Kingdom of Granada, from 1482 to 1492; for sponsoring Columbus's voyages to the Americas; and for expelling the Jews of their kingdoms in 1492 and the Muslims of Castile in 1502.

Johannes Gutenberg: A German goldsmith and most likely the inventor of the printing press; he died c. 1468. Not a single printed book from Gutenberg's time bears his name as publisher, but court records and later chroniclers identify him as the person who, in the early 1450s, created the first printing press. The printing press, which combined the use of movable raised-metal type with a pressing mechanism that applied the inked type to paper, vastly increased the speed and efficiency with which books could be produced.

Jan Hus: A Czech theologian and university professor; born c. 1372, died in 1415. At the University of Prague, where he studied, then taught, Hus became an open defender of the thought and writings of the controversial Oxford theologian John Wycliffe, much to the glee of the Czechs and to the dismay of the Germans at the university. Hus left the University of Prague in 1412 and traveled to the Council of Constance in 1414 to defend himself against accusations that he embraced heretical ideas associated with Wycliffe. In 1415, the Council of Constance condemned Hus as a heretic, and secular authorities burned him at the stake. In 1419, Hus's followers in Bohemia revolted—their revolt, a rare example of a successful revolt staged by a heretical group, continued until 1436.

Joan of Arc: A French peasant and mystic; born c. 1412, died 1431. In 1429, with the Hundred Years War going badly for France and the English besieging the town of Orléans, Joan of Arc visited the French heir to the throne (the *dauphin*), informing him of the religious visions she had experienced and asking that she be allowed to lead a French attempt to relieve Orléans. The *dauphin* allowed Joan to do so, and in 1429, she and her followers broke the English siege of Orléans. Shortly afterward, the *dauphin* felt sufficiently emboldened to have himself crowned as king of France. Joan of Arc continued to lead the French against the English, but she was captured in 1430 and executed for witchcraft by the English in 1431.

William Ockham: An English Franciscan and theologian; born c. 1285, died 1349. William Ockham studied and taught at the University of Oxford until 1324, when he was summoned to Avignon, where his writings were examined for heresy. Ockham's theology, which emphasized divine omnipotence and the logical corollaries of such omnipotence, invited charges that Ockham believed God to be capricious. In 1328, Ockham fled Avignon, ultimately traveling to Munich, where he remained until his death. After leaving Avignon, Ockham abandoned his theological studies and devoted himself to writing about the nature and extent of papal power and denouncing contemporary popes as heretical.

Petrarch/Francesco Petrarca: Italian Humanist; born 1304, died 1374. After abandoning his legal studies in the mid-1320s, Petrarch found employment with an Italian cardinal residing at the papal court of Avignon (he subsequently supported himself through a series of church offices) and devoted himself, as he would for the rest of his life, to his writings and to study of Classical literature. His mastery of Classical Latin, his belief that Classical literature was a better source of moral improvement than Scholastic theology, and his belief that Europe had been mired in a "Dark Age" since the barbarian sack of Rome in 410 all set the stage for the emergence of Humanism and the Italian Renaissance.

Philip IV of France: Known as Philip the Fair; king of France from 1285 to 1314. Philip the Fair's triumphs over a string of popes made manifest the growing strength of the French monarchy, which had been in the ascendant since the 12th century. Philip IV pursued his struggle against Pope Boniface VIII over issues of clerical taxation and supremacy with such intimidating vigor that the successors of Boniface VIII publicly burned some of that pope's bulls. Philip IV's arrest and trial of the Templars, members of a military order supposedly answerable only to the pope, further demonstrated the strength of his position. Before Philip IV's death, popes had taken up residence at Avignon, and even though popes had their own reasons for doing so, contemporaries saw the papal residence at Avignon as evidence of French domination over the papacy.

John Wycliffe: An English theologian and professor at the University of Oxford; born c. 1330, died 1384. Wycliffe became a controversial figure only toward the very end of his life; his close connections to the English royal family shielded him from prosecution. In 1377, the pope condemned 19 articles drawn from one of Wycliffe's treatises; Wycliffe subsequently became more and more outspoken in his criticisms of the contemporary church. Many of Wycliffe's ideas (for example, that all religious beliefs and institutions without explicit scriptural precedent should be abolished and that church property should be seized and redistributed) anticipated the Protestant Reformation. His ideas were embraced by England's first mass heretical movement, the Lollards.

Bibliography

Essential Reading:

Brady, Thomas A., Jr., Heiko Oberman, and James D. Tracy, eds. *Handbook of European History, 1400–1600*, 2 vols. Leiden: E.J. Brill, 1994; republished, Grand Rapids: Wm. B. Eerdmans, 1996. A collection of 40 essays written by experts in their respective fields, providing essential background and bibliography for nearly every aspect of late-medieval history.

Burckhardt, Jacob. *The Civilization of the Renaissance in Italy.* Harmondsworth: Penguin, 1990. Nearly 150 years after its first publication, this book continues to define the terms in which the Renaissance is discussed today.

Bynum, Caroline. *Holy Feast, Holy Fast: The Religious Significance of Food to Medieval Women.* Berkeley and Los Angeles: University of California Press, 1987. Although its subject matter might seem esoteric, this well-written book has enormously influenced how people think about late-medieval religion and the Middle Ages more generally.

Huizinga, Johan. *The Autumn of the Middle Ages*, translated by Rodney J. Payton and Ulrich Mammitzch. Chicago: University of Chicago Press, 1996. *The Waning of the Middle Ages*, translated by F. Hopman. Mineola: Dover Publications, 1998; first published, 1924. Huizinga's 1919 masterpiece has been translated into English twice. The 1996 translation, *The Autumn of the Middle Ages*, has the advantage of being a more complete version of Huizinga's book—the English translation of 1924 was an abridgement. However, the 1924 translation had Huizinga's own approval and input, and some scholars have argued forcefully that the 1924 translation is technically superior to the 1996 translation.

Kristeller, Paul Oskar. *Renaissance Thought and Its Sources.* New York: Columbia University Press, 1979. A definitive guide to Humanist thought, written by one of the greatest 20th-century historians.

Miskimin, Harry. *The Economy of Early Renaissance Europe, 1300–1460.* Englewood Cliffs, NJ: Prentice-Hall, 1969. Still a great introduction to late-medieval economic history.

Oakley, Francis. *The Western Church in the Later Middle Ages.* Ithaca: Cornell University Press, 1978. An authoritative overview of its subject.

Ozment, Steven. *The Age of Reform, 1250–1550*. New Haven: Yale University Press, 1980. This book is the best introduction to late-medieval religious and intellectual history.

Tuchman, Barbara. *A Distant Mirror: The Calamitous Fourteenth Century*. New York: Alfred A. Knopf, 1978. This book is "essential reading" by virtue of its wide readership and high profile.

Supplementary Reading:

Aberth, John, ed. *The Black Death. The Great Mortality of 1348–1350: A Brief History with Documents*. New York: Bedford/St. Martin's, 2005. This book is perhaps the best place to start for those with an interest in the Black Death. The author's treatment of the many controversies surrounding the history of the Black Death is sober-minded and judicious.

Allmand, Christopher. *The Hundred Years War: England and France at War, c. 1300–c. 1450*. Cambridge: Cambridge University Press, 1988. This book takes a more analytical approach to the war than does Sumption's (listed below) and, therefore, complements that book nicely.

Astell, Ann, and Bonnie Wheeler, eds. *Joan of Arc and Spirituality*. New York: Palgrave Macmillan, 2003. The illuminating essays in this collection offer new insights into the impact of Joan of Arc on both her contemporaries and modern individuals.

Babinger, Franz. *Mehmed II and His Time*, translated by Ralph Manheim. Princeton: Princeton University Press, 1978. First published in German in 1958, this classic biography remains as gripping as ever.

Barber, Malcolm. *The Trial of the Templars*, 2nd ed. Cambridge: Cambridge University Press, 2006. The best scholarly account of an event that has occasioned some very imaginative, not to say unhinged, historical writing.

Benedictow, Ole. *The Black Death, 1346–1353: The Complete History*. Woodbridge, U.K., and Rochester, NY: Boydell, 2004. Not the most humbly titled book, but it does bring together a vast amount of information.

Bentley, Jerry. *Humanists and Holy Writ: New Testament Scholarship in the Renaissance*. Princeton: Princeton University Press, 1983. A good, traditional work of intellectual history.

Bisaha, Nancy. *Creating East and West: Renaissance Humanists and the Ottoman Turks*. Philadelphia: University of Philadelphia Press, 2004. An intriguing study of how Westerners perceived the Ottomans and, thereby, defined themselves.

Blumenfeld-Kosinski, Renate. *Poets, Saints, and Visionaries of the Great Schism, 1378–1417*. University Park: Penn State University Press, 2006. A readable and thoughtful study of how contemporaries understood and reacted to the Great Papal Schism.

Broedel, Hans Peter. *Malleus Maleficarum and the Construction of Witchcraft: Theology and Popular Belief*. Manchester: Manchester University Press, 2003. An admirably clear discussion of the chief late-medieval witch-hunting manual and of the two men who wrote it.

Brucker, Gene. *Renaissance Florence*. Berkeley and Los Angeles: University of California Press, 1969. This book places the Renaissance in its Florentine context; a wonderful overview.

Bull, Marcus. *Thinking Medieval: An Introduction to the Study of the Middle Ages*. New York: Palgrave Macmillan, 2005. Sheds light on how the Middle Ages is represented in popular culture and on the period's significance in the modern world.

Burke, Peter. *The Italian Renaissance*, 2nd ed. Princeton: Princeton University Press, 1999. A thoughtful attempt to answer the biggest questions associated with the rise of the Italian Renaissance.

Burr, David. *The Spiritual Franciscans: From Persecution to Protest in the Century after Saint Francis*. University Park: Pennsylvania State University Press, 2001. A great general history of the Spiritual Franciscan movement and the opposition it faced from critics and inquisitors.

Cohen, Kathleen. *Metamorphosis of a Death Symbol: The Transi Tomb in the Late Middle Ages*. Berkeley and Los Angeles: University of California Press, 1973. The best study of a phenomenon that continues to color our understanding of the period.

Cohn, Samuel Kline. *The Laboring Classes in Renaissance Florence*. New York: Academic Press, 1980. An important contribution to our understanding of the revolt of the *Ciompi* and its Florentine context.

Contamine, Philippe. *War in the Middle Ages*. New York: Blackwell, 1984. Authoritative and scholarly overview of the subject and very useful for the Late Middle Ages.

Cook, Noble David. *Born to Die: Disease and the New World Conquest, 1492–1650*. Cambridge: Cambridge University Press, 1998. Wonderfully illustrates how crucial European diseases were in the conquest of the New World.

Crosby, Alfred W. *The Columbian Exchange: Biological and Cultural Consequences of 1492 (30ᵗʰ Anniversary Edition)*. Westport: Praeger, 2003. The classic account of its subject.

Curry, Anne. *The Hundred Years War*, 2ⁿᵈ ed. New York: Palgrave Macmillan, 2003. A comprehensive look at this historical period.

Daileader, Philip. *True Citizens: Violence, Memory, and Identity in the Medieval Community of Perpignan, 1162–1397*. Leiden: Brill, 2000. Attempts, among other things, to assess how mindsets did and did not change during the course of the 14ᵗʰ century.

Dewald, Jonathan. *The European Nobility, 1400 to 1800*. Cambridge: Cambridge University Press, 1996. The best short introduction to its subject; invaluable for understanding how nobles reacted to adverse circumstances.

Dickens, A. G., ed. *The Courts of Europe: Politics, Patronage, and Royalty, 1400–1800*. New York: McGraw Hill, 1977. Helps put the European court system in a broader historical context.

Duffy, Eamon. *The Stripping of the Altars: Traditional Religion in England, 1400–1580*. New Haven: Yale University Press, 1992. Argues against the notion that late-medieval religion was decadent or dysfunctional.

Edwards, John. *Ferdinand and Isabella*. New York: Longman, 2005. Short and superb introduction to two of the most important rulers in late-medieval Europe.

Eisenstein, Elizabeth. *The Printing Press as an Agent of Change*, 2 vols. Cambridge: Cambridge University Press, 1979. Argues strongly that the printing press revolutionized European culture and thought.

Epstein, Steven. *Wage Labor and Guilds in Medieval Europe*. Chapel Hill: University of North Carolina Press, 1991. To understand the medieval economy, you have to understand the guild system, and this book provides a fine introduction to that system.

Fernández-Armesto, Felipe. *Before Columbus: Exploration and Colonization from the Mediterranean to the Atlantic, 1229–1492*. Philadelphia: University of Pennsylvania Press, 1987. A very readable overview of a subject whose significance is insufficiently recognized.

Fourquin, Guy. *The Anatomy of Popular Rebellion in the Middle Ages*. Amsterdam: North Holland Publishing, 1978. A sociological and historical examination of late-medieval revolutions.

Freedman, Paul H. *Images of the Medieval Peasant*. Stanford: Stanford University Press, 1998. Essential reading for understanding the place of peasants in medieval society and culture.

Füssel, Stephen. *Gutenberg and the Impact of Printing*. Aldershot and Burlington: Ashgate, 2005. An excellent introduction to Gutenberg and printing; especially strong on the history of printing in the two generations after Gutenberg's death.

Geremek, Bronislaw. *The Margins of Society in Late Medieval Paris*. Cambridge: Cambridge University Press, 1979. A pioneering work of late-medieval social history.

Goldthwaite, Richard. *Wealth and the Demand for Art in Italy*. Baltimore: Johns Hopkins University Press, 1993. A challenging but important book that links the Italian Renaissance to the emergence of a consumer culture.

Grafton, Anthony. *Commerce with the Classics: Ancient Books and Renaissance Readers*. Ann Arbor: University of Michigan Press, 1987. A colorful examination of how Renaissance readers engaged with ancient texts.

———, and Lisa Jardine. *From Humanism to the Humanities: Education and the Liberal Arts in Fifteenth- and Sixteenth-Century Europe*. Cambridge: Harvard University Press, 1986. A quirky but enlightening examination of how Humanism was practiced in the classroom.

———, April Shelford, and Nancy Siraisi. *New Worlds, Ancient Texts: The Power of Tradition and the Shock of Discovery*. Cambridge: Harvard University Press, 1992. This book describes, in vivid detail, the effect of the New World's discovery on previously held notions of life outside of Europe.

Guenée, Bernard. *States and Rulers in Later Medieval Europe*, translated by Juliet Vale. New York: Blackwell, 1985. A thorough discussion of how the nature and institutions of government changed.

Hanawalt, Barbara. *The Ties That Bound: Peasant Families in Medieval England*. Oxford: Oxford University Press, 1986. Argues for the stability of family life during a period usually known for its turbulence and for the similarity between medieval and modern families; makes remarkable use of coroner reports to re-create late-medieval life.

Hilton, Rodney. *Bond Men Made Free: Medieval Peasant Movements and the English Rising of 1381*. New York: Routledge, 2003. First published in

1973, this book places the English Peasants Revolt in a broad geographical and chronological context.

Hirsch, Rudolf. *Printing, Selling, and Reading, 1450–1550*, 2nd ed. Wiesbaden: Otto Harrassowitz, 1974. Loaded with valuable information about the first century of European printing.

Homza, LuAnn, ed. *The Spanish Inquisition: An Anthology of Sources, 1478–1614*. Indianapolis: Hackett, 2006. Perhaps the best place for those with an interest in the Spanish Inquisition to begin; provides a pithy history of that institution. The accompanying documents (which constitute the heart of the book) are well worth reading.

Housley, Norman. *The Later Crusades, 1274–1580: From Lyons to Alcazar*. Oxford: Oxford University Press, 1992. Scholarly in the best sense of the word—a magisterial overview.

Hudson, Anne. *The Premature Reformation: Wycliffite Texts and Lollard History*. Oxford: Oxford University Press, 1988. An interesting and level-headed examination of the relationship between Wycliffe and the Lollards.

Jansen, Katherine. *The Making of the Magdalen: Preaching and Popular Devotion in the Later Middle Ages*. Princeton: Princeton University Press, 2000. An original examination of an important aspect of late-medieval religiosity.

Jordan, William. *The Great Famine: Northern Europe in the Early Fourteenth Century*. Princeton: Princeton University Press, 1996. A solid account of the conditions that led up to the Great Famine and a gold mine of interesting information about the early 14th century.

Kafadar, Cemal. *Between Two Worlds: The Construction of the Ottoman State*. Berkeley and Los Angeles: University of California Press, 1995. A sophisticated and thought-provoking examination of the emergence of the Ottomans and of modern scholarship devoted to that phenomenon.

Kamen, Henry. *Spain, 1469–1714: A Society of Conflict*, 3rd ed. New York: Longman, 2005. Explores the ascent and decline of Spain as a world power, along with the political and social conflicts central to this period.

———. *The Spanish Inquisition: A Historical Revision*. New Haven: Yale University Press, 1998. The best extended account of the Spanish Inquisition, although critics have suggested—sometimes, but not always, justifiably so—that the author's attempts to cut the Spanish Inquisition down to size go too far. This version of Kamen's book is greatly superior to the first, which appeared in the 1960s.

Kaminsky, Howard. *A History of the Hussite Revolution*. Berkeley and Los Angeles: University of California Press, 1967. A thorough and detailed account of the Hussites.

Kapr, Albert. *Johann Gutenberg: The Man and His Invention*. Aldershot and Brookfield: Ashgate, 1996. With its more detailed examination of Gutenberg's life and German milieu, this book nicely complements Füssel's (see above).

Kaye, Joel. *Economy and Nature in the Fourteenth Century: Money, Market Exchange, and the Emergence of Scientific Thought*. Cambridge: Cambridge University Press, 1998. A bold study arguing that the monetization of the European economy caused 14th-century thinkers to approach physics in an increasingly quantitative manner, a move that, in turn, anticipated the later Scientific Revolution.

Keen, Maurice. *Chivalry*. New Haven: Yale University Press, 1984. A key text to understanding the history and influence of this social concept.

Kenny, Anthony. *Wyclif*. Oxford University Press, 1985. A very good, brief introduction.

Kieckhefer, Richard. *European Witch Trials: Their Foundations in Popular and Learned Culture, 1300–1500*. Berkeley and Los Angeles: University of California Press, 1976. Still the best survey of witch trials in late-medieval Europe—thoroughly researched.

King, Margaret L. *Women of the Renaissance*. Chicago: University of Chicago Press, 1991. A very readable extended essay on women and the family, the church, and high culture.

Lambert, Malcolm. *Medieval Heresy: Popular Movements from the Gregorian Reform to the Reformation*, 3rd ed. New York: Blackwell, 2002. A comprehensive look at history's heretical movements and what they say about the Middle Ages.

Lehfeldt, Elizabeth A., ed. *The Black Death*. Boston: Houghton Mifflin, 2005. This book handily brings together excerpts from 20 important modern historical works that examine the Black Death from various viewpoints.

Liss, Peggy K. *Isabel the Queen: Life and Times*, rev. ed. Philadelphia: University of Philadelphia Press, 2004. A good scholarly study that provides more detail than Edwards's more general book (listed above.)

Luongo, Thomas. *The Saintly Politics of Catherine of Siena*. Ithaca: Cornell University Press, 2006. Luongo's scholarly look at the influential medieval saint emphasizes her practical side.

Mate, Mavis E. *Daughters, Wives and Widows after the Black Death: Women in Sussex, 1350–1535*. Woodbridge, U.K.: Boydell Press, 1998. A detailed study of the economic consequences of the Black Death for women, emphasizing the complexity of those consequences—the sort of book that academics tend to like better than general readers do.

McSheffrey, Shannon. *Gender and Heresy: Women and Men in Lollard Communities, 1420–1530*. Philadelphia: University of Pennsylvania Press, 1995. A good example of how a consideration of gender can provide a new perspective on a familiar subject.

Menache, Sophia. *Clement V*. Cambridge: Cambridge University Press, 1998. Contains a wealth of information on the Avignon pontificate.

Molho, Anthony. "The Italian Renaissance, Made in the USA." In *Imagined Histories: American Historians Interpret the Past*, edited by Anthony Molho and Gordon S. Wood, pp. 263-294. Princeton: Princeton University Press, 1998. A wonderful essay on the relationship between Americans and the Renaissance; part of a collection of essays that explore the past from an American point of view.

Mollat, Michel, and Philippe Wolff. *The Popular Revolutions of the Late Middle Ages*. London: Allen & Unwin, 1973. Perhaps the best introduction to the subject.

Naphy, William, and Andrew Spicer. *Plague: Black Death and Pestilence in Europe*. Gloucestershire, U.K.: Tempus Publishing, 2004. Essential reading for an understanding of this defining event in the history of medieval Europe.

Nichol, Donald M. *The End of the Byzantine Empire*. New York: Holmes & Meier, 1979. A brief and very readable account of the Byzantine Empire's last years.

———. *The Last Centuries of Byzantium, 1261–1453*, 2nd ed. Cambridge: Cambridge University Press, 1993. A solid overview of the revival and final collapse of the Byzantine Empire.

Nirenberg, David. *Communities of Violence: The Persecution of Minorities in the Middle Ages*. Princeton: Princeton University Press, 1996. A sophisticated and rewarding study of the persecution of Jews and Muslims in 14th-century Catalonia and southern France.

Oakley, Francis. *The Conciliarist Tradition: Constitutionalism in the Catholic Church, 1300–1870.* Oxford: Oxford University Press, 2003. Places conciliarism in a broad historical context.

Oberman, Heiko L. *The Harvest of Medieval Theology: Gabriel Biel and Late Medieval Nominalism.* Cambridge: Harvard University Press, 1963. An influential study that seeks to demonstrate that late-medieval Scholasticism, far from being sterile, remained a vibrant field.

Pernoud, Régine, and Marie-Véronique Clin. *Joan of Arc: Her Story.* New York: St. Martin's, 1998. A stunning look at Joan of Arc's life and character.

Peters, Edward. *The Witch, the Magician, and the Law.* Philadelphia: University of Pennsylvania Press, 1978. A fine overview of how canon law treated magic and magicians during the Middle Ages.

Phillips, William D., Jr., and Carla Rahn Phillips. *The Worlds of Christopher Columbus.* Cambridge: Cambridge University Press, 1992. An excellent, dispassionate treatment of a subject that tends to generate heated diatribes.

Prestwich, Michael. *Armies and Warfare in the Middle Ages: The English Experience.* New Haven: Yale University Press, 1996. Provides a thorough account of how warfare was enacted in Medieval Europe.

Renouard, Yves. *The Avignon Papacy, 1305–1403.* New York: Barnes & Noble 1994; first published, 1954. A good, short introduction to the 14th-century papacy.

Ruiz, Teofilo. *Spanish Society, 1400–1600.* New York: Longman, 2001. A fascinating account of Spanish society, with an emphasis on social ritual and how it changed over time.

Rummel, Erika. *The Humanist-Scholastic Debate in the Renaissance and Reformation.* Cambridge: Harvard University Press, 1986. Provides a fine overview of the nuances of that debate.

Russell, Peter. *Prince Henry the Navigator.* New Haven: Yale University Press, 2000. This book reminds us—as if we needed such reminding—why biography remains such a popular genre. Great reading.

Russell-Wood, A. J. R. *The Portuguese Empire, 1415–1808: A World on the Move.* Baltimore: Johns Hopkins University Press, 1998. Takes a thematic approach to its subject—highly recommended.

Scott, Karen. "Mystical Death, Bodily Death: Catherine of Siena and Raymond of Capua on the Mystic's Encounter with God." In *Gendered*

Voices: Medieval Saints and Their Interpreters, edited by Catherine M. Mooney, pp. 136–167. Philadelphia: University of Pennsylvania Press, 1999. An academic article that tries to reconcile two differing interpretations of Catherine of Siena's life.

———. "St. Catherine of Siena, 'Apostola.'" *Church History* 61 (1992): 34–46. An engrossing article about the medieval saint.

Smoller, Laura Ackerman. *History, Prophecy, and the Stars: The Christian Astrology of Pierre d'Ailly, 1350–1420*. Princeton: Princeton University Press, 1994. An interesting study of a late-medieval theologian's mental world, set in the context of the Great Schism.

Spade, Paul Vincent. *The Cambridge Companion to Ockham*. Cambridge: Cambridge University Press, 1999. Helps non-specialists come to grips with the complexity of Ockham's thought.

Spinka, Matthew. *John Hus: A Biography*. Princeton: Princeton University Press, 1968. A thorough biography of this influential thinker and philosopher.

Strayer, Joseph. *The Reign of Philip the Fair*. Princeton: Princeton University Press, 1980. A classic work of royal biography and administrative history.

Sumption, Jonathan. *The Hundred Years War*, 2 vols. to date. London: Faber and Faber, 1990, 1999. Narrative history written in the grand old style; great reading. Currently published volumes cover the period to 1369; future volumes will take the story further.

Tierney, Brian. *Foundations of the Conciliar Theory*. Cambridge: Cambridge University Press, 1955. A classic work essential for any scholar of late-medieval religion.

Van Engen, John, ed. *The Past and Future of Medieval Studies*. South Bend, IN: University of Notre Dame Press, 1994. Paints a picture of how the study of the Middle Ages has evolved in academia.

Wheeler, Bonnie, ed. *Fresh Verdicts on Joan of Arc*. New York: Garland, 1996. A collection of insightful essays that serves as a welcome introduction for those interested in learning more about Joan of Arc.

Willard, Charity Cannon. *Christine de Pizan: Her Life and Works*. New York: Persea, 1984. The best place to start for those wanting to know more about this important late-medieval author.

Notes